Indian H[...]

The ultimate cookbook to prepare over 100 delicious, traditional and modern Indian recipes to spice up your meals

By

Adele Tyler

© **Copyright 2020 by Adele Tayler - All rights reserved.**

This document is geared towards providing exact and reliable information in regards to the topic and issue covered. The publication is sold with the idea that the publisher is not required to render accounting, officially permitted, or otherwise, qualified services. If advice is necessary, legal or professional, a practiced individual in the profession should be ordered.

- From a Declaration of Principles which was accepted and approved equally by a Committee of the American Bar Association and a Committee of Publishers and Associations.

In no way is it legal to reproduce, duplicate, or transmit any part of this document in either electronic means or in printed format. Recording of this publication is strictly prohibited and any storage of this document is not allowed unless with written permission from the publisher. All rights reserved.

The information provided herein is stated to be truthful and consistent, in that any liability, in terms of inattention or otherwise, by any usage or abuse of any policies, processes, or directions contained within is the solitary and utter responsibility of the recipient reader. Under no circumstances will any legal responsibility or blame be held against the publisher for any reparation, damages, or monetary loss due to the information herein, either directly or indirectly.

Respective authors own all copyrights not held by the publisher.

The information herein is offered for informational purposes solely, and is universal as so. The presentation of the information is without contract or any type of guarantee assurance.

The trademarks that are used are without any consent, and the publication of the trademark is without permission or backing by the trademark owner.

All trademarks and brands within this book are for clarifying purposes only and are the owned by the owners themselves, not affiliated with this document.

Table of Contents

INTRODUCTION 5

CHAPTER 01: LEARNING THE BASICS OF INDIAN CUISINE 14

1.1 Indian Regional Foods - at a Glance 14

1.2 Features of Indian Food 19

1.3 Essentials of Indian Foods in your Diet and Its Benefits 20

1.4 Health Benefits of Consuming Indian Food 26

1.5 How is Home Cooked Indian Food Different from Restaurant Food?
....27

CHAPTER 02: COMMON SPICES USED IN INDIAN CUISINE AND THEIR PROPERTIES 30

CHAPTER 03: INDIAN BREAKFAST RECIPES 38

CHAPTER 04: INDIAN LUNCH AND DINNER RECIPES ...64

CHAPTER 05: INDIAN DESSERT RECIPES 84

CHAPTER 06: VEGETARIAN INDIAN RECIPES 99

CONCLUSION 106

Introduction

India, South Asia's great area of land, is host to one of the largest and most powerful civilizations in the world. We are all quite mindful of the fact that the Indians are quite foodie. We always wish to speak about cooking, to eat and to try various recipes. Certainly, each and every single household in India has its own formula which they elevate from generation to generation. Yet, how much are we really conscious of Indian food history? Thus, the Indian Food Heritage journey will be discussed in this topic.

India has received a multitude of immigrants with a number of religious traditions through more than 4,000 years of recorded history.

To understand the dynamics of India's native food culture, one has to know that this nation is far from culturally homogeneous.

Regions and sects make up a great deal of the food. "Indian food" was invented a term that a native will probably chuckle at because such a word would be like saying "North American wine" to a wine expert.

There are many places in India that have their own special cooking methods, seasonings, and fresh ingredients. Tipping its population-scale to over a billion, its food diversity is as diverse as its inhabitants.

Muslims and Hindu are the two dominant sects that most affected Indian food culture and food choices. They took out their own food practices with each movement of natives. There is the widespread practice of the vegetarian Hindu culture. In comparison, Muslim culture is the most common in meat cooking. Mughlai cuisine, kababs, nargisi kaftas, biryani and favorite dishes served in the tandoor are great benefits provided by Muslim natives in India. The food in South India is mostly rice related, with a thin porridge accent named Rasam. In all South Indian cuisine, coconut is an essential component. Dosa and idli are very common foods among vegetarian from Hindu culture. Also, the Portuguese, Persians, and British contributed a great deal too Indian food. The British brought tea to India, and it is nowadays the favorite drink of many Indians.

The four main geographic types of Indian cooking are the North, East, South, and West. North India was impacted by the Mughal dynasty which held power for 300 years until they were substituted by the British in the 18th century. Naan bread, produced in a tandoor, is not native. It is the Afghani people's daily meal. Naan is not Indians' baked daily bread, but it has been a common misconception of Indian food outside the region for decades.

Among Southern Indians, specified steamed rice cakes are favorite. Rice is consumed in all meals, and lunch mostly consists of all meal courses, each filled with rice again. The Hindus are categorized into vegetarians and non-vegetarians. Their common thread in Kerala's Southern Region is coconut, which is the state's culinary mascot.

The Gujarat, Maharashtra and Goa western states all have unique experiences of health. Gujarat has predominantly Muslims, Hindus, Parsis and Jains who have their own cooking methods. Parsis have a rich diet of poultry and seafood. Gujaratis are primarily veggie eaters, and Gujarat is known as one of the best places for consuming vegetarian food. Maharashtra is a large state with its Mumbai city of fame. East states are very distinct. Bengali cuisine, with fish and rice at the core of the diet, can be characterized as delicate and subtle. The order of a Bengali meal starts with a mixed vegetable dish with a bitter taste and finishes with a rich sweet dessert based on milk for which Bengali is popular. Orissa is popular for squash blossoms rolled in rice and deep-fried paste or turned into patties. Cod and other fish are in the diet too. It is very rare that chicken will be eaten here, and poultry plays a small culinary role in general. Bihar and Jharkhand love their vegetables and beans, but with their diet, they do have Western overtones like beef, pork, goat and poultry. Indian cuisine tends to be unified only by its locality from East to West, but its taste is evidently boundless.

Brief History of Traditional Indian Dishes

The past of Indian food is the background of innovation from various societies in periods of need and succession. Such dishes were created for general populous sake, while others have been imported from all over the geographies. Many of those fascinating Indian food tales are now unaware of. Some of the Traditional Indian is explained as below:

- **Petha is older than Taj Mahal**

Petha in Agra is the best choice to consume. The innovation is relevant to the development of the Taj Mahal in the Mughals. When the monumental shrine was under a building, the daily meal containing just dal and roti bored some 20,000 employees. Then Mughal Emperor Shah Jahan expressed his worry with the master architect Ustad Isa Effendi who demanded a response to the Emperor's problems from Pir Naqshbandi Sahib. It is claimed that one day, during prayers, the Pir formed a trance and gave Petha's formula to Mughal. About 500 cooks then rendered Petha for the staff.

- **Dal Bati Was a Tool of Survival in Wars**

This is Rajasthan's best food to eat. The recipe of Dal Bati is a tale worth sharing with. This Rajasthani food has its roots in the popular Mewar Chittorgarh Fort. Bati is wheat dough fried in oil, a food that the Mewar Rajput kings needed to live in unfavorable wartime circumstances. Bati could be produced in the desert lands of Rajasthan with the few supplies and a little water available.

- **Mysore Went from Monarchy to Common**

It is South India's, iconic sweetmeat. The past of Mysore is related to the Mysore Palace kitchen of the early 20th century. In the Mysore Palace, the royal cook used to impress the King with numerous dishes. He rendered a new sweet dish one day with the mixture of chickpea flour, oil and sugar. The cook coined the word 'Mysore Paka' in a split second on being questioned the word of the sauce. 'Paka' is a Kannada word which signifies a sweet mixture.

- **Khaja is Generational of the Mauryan and Gupta Realms**

While the cooking art of creating Khaja is a moment of honor for the Orissa citizens, it is claimed that the technique was borrowed from Bihar's central highlands around 2200 years ago. Khaja's roots go back to antique Indian Gupta empires. Rajgir's Khaja in Bihar is famed for its swelling, while Kakinada's Khaja in Andhra Pradesh is popular for its dry outside but savory within.

- **Jalebi's Culture is Not Necessarily Indian**

One of India's most famous sweet dishes, Jalebi owes its roots to West Asia. Jalebi was introduced to India in mediaeval times by the Persian-speaking invaders. This sweetmeat was called 'Kundalika' in India in the 14th century, and 'Jalavallika'. During Ramadan in Iran, the poor were given platefuls of Jalebi.

- **Dum Biryani Provided Meals in Awadh for the Needy**

According to numerous historical records, the root of biryani is the provincial capital of Hyderabad in the Nawab period. Some discussions show that biryani was initiated in the early mediaeval era during Timur's invasion of India. While biryani's origin is being discussed, Dum Biryani or Awadh's Biryani emerged in Lucknow. The Nawab of Awadh directed all the poor folks of his area to cook a meal in big handis (round-shaped brass pots) when food was scarce. A large volume of food was cooked in covered and sealed pans, with limited energy. This cooking craft has been popular as 'dum'.

Indian Food and Its Popularity in the US

Indian food is becoming increasingly common in the US. It is like a highly specialized food right now.

Apart from Chinese cuisine, which is almost part of the American environment, the food network shows even more references of Indian cuisine and Indian ingredients are showing up everywhere in the US. Thanks to their wonderful taste, Indian dishes have earned popularity around the world. Several tasty Indian meals are cooked in different dining spots around the country. Various fans on a global scale have noticed the vast range of salads, appetizers, sweets, side dishes and desserts, as Indian restaurants have been expanded at an unprecedented pace, with immense popularity in every imaginable community and in every imaginable corner of the Globe.

India is the world's largest grocer of fruit. India has tremendous science and engineering potential that is rapidly being used to produce modern, popular food goods in the US. New products are still in demand, so there is tremendous potential for new products, especially in the US, where people love to eat Indian food. The success of American Indian food has also enabled a movement for Indian businesses to sell more food products to the US.

Indian cuisine is known in the world for its spices and aromatic taste. The numerous Indian restaurants in Washington DC prepare mouth-watering dishes and serve it to both the visitors and the local people in the region. Every place has unique culinary art, which is completely different from each other. These techniques were introduced to western countries and acquired enormous prominence among citizens. For special occasions, the special dish is cooked. Many international buyers have been fascinated by the spices and the different products used to cook such dishes.

It is very important to remember that there is a therapeutic benefit in most Indian spices. The most widely used herbs are turmeric, ginger and cardamom since they have therapeutic properties.

This is one of the key explanations, why citizens in the US are sincerely willing to consume Indian food, claiming that the Indian food would not affect their body in any way as the spices used, have medicinal properties. In this book, you will learn the Indian Cuisine, spices often used in them, and 100 recipes, in detail.

Chapter 01: Learning the Basics of Indian Cuisine

Indian cuisine is comprised of a number of modern and conventional Indian subcontinent cuisines. Owing to the variety of land, climate, history, ethnic groups, and professions, these foods differ considerably and use herbs, vegetables, and fruits available locally. Also, Indian food is highly related to religion, particularly Hinduism, social decisions and rituals.

1.1 Indian Regional Foods - at a Glance

While presenting dishes as part of a standardized, nationalized cuisine is popular for Indian restaurants. India's food is actually as regionally unique and diverse as its people. These foods are hugely affected by the past of India, it is trading relations, and it is cultural and religious traditions. A little context on the commonalities and variations between the regional cuisines of India will transform your next Indian meal into an entertaining, and profoundly gratifying.

While Indian food is highly local unique, there are some popular ties that connect the numerous cuisine practices. Indian cuisine across the nation is highly reliant on sauces, which are sauce-like sauce or soup-like meat, potato, or cheese dishes. However, the unique spice mixtures, liquidity amount, and ingredients are decided by regional choice. In general, Indian cuisine is also highly dependent upon agriculture, while Southern Indian areas use rice more strongly than other places. Both regional foods depend on legumes or "pulses." Indian cuisine can use a wider range of peas than any other menu selections: Red lentils, black gram, peas or yellow gramme, black gramme, and green gramme are used in a variety of Indian dishes as a whole, broken, or ground in flour. Add tartness to meals that do not use eggs, legumes, and nutrition to vegan diets.

The rich usage of spices is probably the most distinguishing feature of Indian food. Indian spice blends mostly use up to five separate spices, occasionally adding ten or more. Garam masala is a common mixture of spices, cardamom, cinnamon, and clove, with the specific spices differing by area and personal recipe.

✤ Observations Indicated: Commerce and Invasion

In India's cuisine, the cultural effect of trade is clear, with unique areas and dishes carrying the sign of international influence. Arab and Canadian traders strongly desired India's spices; in return, India obtained several commodities that profoundly shaped its food heritage. Portuguese merchants carried in New World products such as onions, peppers, and chilies, which were profoundly incorporated into Indian dishes. Coffee was carried by Arab merchants.

India's occupation times have also significantly influenced the nature of its delicacies. Mughal conquerors, who ruled India between both the early 1500s and late 1600s, introduced Persian spices and traditions in India's culinary culture.

The influence is noticeable in the use of cheese and milk in sauces, the use of meat and nuts in salads, and in particular in salads.

Although the arrival of the British in India exposed the nation to soup and tea; it had no effect on its food. However, the imperial incorporation of local food into British society has profoundly influenced Indian food translation abroad. Tikka Masala, a flavorful sauce on many Indian menus, is originally an Anglo-Indian invention and is widely called as "Britain's true national dish". Even European conceptions of Indian "curry"-the term applies to a myriad of garlicky and stew-like meals-are inferred from British understanding of Indian cuisine.

India: Large Community

The population of India is incredibly complex, with cultural traditions deeply shaped by ethnic and religious specificities. Ayurvedic traditions also exercised control on Indian cuisine in particular by trying to dictate spice combinations and cooking methods, stressing the balance between brain, body, and spirit. This theory is a popular influence in Indian cuisine, as per religion and cultural characteristics. Around one-third of the population in India is vegetarian, determined by its Hindu, Jain or Buddhist values. Consequently, a large portion of the countrywide Indian dishes is without beef. In addition, religious traditions influence other dietary prohibitions that form India's cuisine: Hindu believers abstain from meat, since cattle are holy in this religion, whereas Muslims claim that pork is impure and they never eat it. Depending on a region's prevailing religious beliefs, cooking in a given area can exclude those ingredients to conform to religious rules.

⁜ Northern Indian Kitchen

Northern Indian cuisine, possibly the most widespread cuisine form found from outside India, demonstrates a clear Mughal influence. It is distinguished by strong dairy consumption: milk, paneer (a mild Indian cheese), butter, and yoghurt are all commonly used in Northern dishes. A famous Northern treat is samosas and sometimes beef. Clay ovens identified as tandoors are common in the North, offering their distinct barbecue flavor to dishes such as naan. A considerable number of Northern foods appear daily on Indian menus. Dal or Paneer Makhani is common vegetarian dishes, comprising of dal or paneer fried in a creamy tomato sauce, oignons, mango dust, and curry powder. Korma, another Northern Indian staple meal, is a smooth curry with coconut milk or yoghurt, cumin, cilantro and tiny quantities of cashews or walnuts. It can be eaten with numerous meats, typically poultry or lamb, but often beef and a vegan dish with paneer.

⁜ West Indian Kitchen

Western local food is characterized by its region's political and cultural particularities. The coastal area of Maharashtra is known for their milk-dominant seafood and coconut cuisine. Gujarati food is mainly vegetarian, and due to strong influences, has an inherent sweetness to most of its dishes. Since this region's dry climate reported to be low veggies, this region is well renowned for its chutneys, common Indian condiments which use fried, fresh, or marinated fruits and vegetables with sweet, sour, or spicy flavors. Goa served as a large port and colony of commerce for Portugal, culminating in a rare mix of Indian and Portuguese cuisine features. Goa cuisine utilizes more commonly than other different foods in India, utilizing beef and pork. Vinegar is also a distinctive component in Goa cuisine. Its coastal presence results in the proliferation of coconut milk, coconut powder and fish in Goa cuisine.

✤ East Indian Kitchen

Eastern local food is renowned mainly for their sweets. Not only are these desserts preferred by other states of India, but they are also found in restaurants. Their delicate sweet is rendering an outstanding finale to dinner. Rasgulla is a common sweet treat, consisting of balls of semolina and cheese curd, boiled in light sugar syrup. Eastern dishes prefer mustard seeds and mustard oil, bringing a pleasant smell to the dishes. In Eastern cuisine rice and seafood are also prominent. Eastern foods, on the whole, are spiced more strongly than from certain countries.

✤ Indian Southern Food

Southern Indian food is not usually seen on many menus of restaurants and is somewhat distinct from other areas. Their "curries" vary greatly in their appearance and may usually be classified as per the drier quality, or those preferring a more stew-like or soupy appearance. Poriyals, dried curries made up of a mixture of veggies and seasoning, complement the rice food. Sambars are basically pea and vegetable stews with a tamarind taste, which are soupier than curries from many other countries, but smoother than rasams. Rasams in their quality is somewhat comparable to soups, and comprise mostly of tomatoes, tamarind, and a variety of spices. Kootus is more comparable to curries seen in other regions, but instead of being fluffy like the North's dairy-based curries, kootus gets its strength from drained lentils.

Southern Indian food is renowned for its exquisite fried or griddle-cooked sweets, in addition to curry-style dishes. Dosas consist of a broad crepe. They are normally packed with curries of veggies, curries, or seasonings. Idli is fried delicacy identical to savory doughnuts, which are eaten as sambar and rasam side dishes.

Apart from restaurants directly serving Southern Indian cuisine, pappadams, fried crispy rice cookies commonly spiced with black peppercorns, are the only South Indian food that are often seen in Indian restaurants.

1.2 Features of Indian Food

Indian food has penetrated all territorial frontiers and entered the international territory. Everyone seems to recognize and love the Tandoori chicken or the Pav bhaji or the Kesar kulfi today. Foodies worldwide are massive fans of both vegetarian and non-vegetarian Indian delicacies.

- **The Pattern Present**

More and more customers are visiting the world's prestigious Indian restaurants and eating famous Indian culinary delights. In the food chain, Indian food is growing rapidly by the day. Tandoori is strongly in request all over the world. North Indian food is extremely delicious. The wonderful Tandoori snacks like the Tandoori Chicken Chicken Reshmi Kebabs and much more you will never get over.

- **Astonishing Richness**

Owing to its exceptional variety Indian food is becoming famous over the years. Indian food has plenty for any form of taste bud to satisfy. Some citizens are interested in South Indian delicacies; some are intrigued by Punjabi delights, some are obsessed with Rajasthani or Goa food, Parsi food or mouth-watering Bengali foods. A new life has been granted to Indian street food by adding a few fusion variants.

- **Food the Unstoppable Ratio**

Most Indian foods are cooked in such a way that the nutritious content of all the products is preserved and is not compromised due to the cooking method.

Indian cuisine gets its true experience and tastes owing to a number of spices. These spices are good for the skin. It offers pickles and greens in various parts of India. Their flavors are special to the area, but they can activate your taste buds.

1.3 Essentials of Indian Foods in your Diet and Its Benefits

Taking into account considerations, we have arranged an important Indian food that must be part of every diet. Remember that if you are struggling from any health condition, please ask your doctor what you can take from this chart and cannot.

- **Fruits**

Many typical fruits of Indian heritage are perfect for you. They include all sorts of essential vitamins and minerals which are important to us. You can consume daily seasonal and annual fruits, such as strawberries, bananas, pomegranates, pineapples, etc. People with such health problems ought to avoid certain fruits but, for the normal citizen, these are the ideal healthy food that can supplement the fried chip bag. Health advantages Fruits provides:

- Fruits are suppliers of various under-consumed vital nutrients, including calcium, dietary fiber and vitamin C.
- Typically most fruits are poor in sugar, salt and energy.
- As you consume fruit, the energy production rises in no time; it is one of the fruit's main advantages that we can include in our hectic schedules.
- Not only does the fiber content in the fruit have a genius relaxing effect, but it also helps you feel complete when incorporating bulk protein to your diet.

↓ Chilies

New chilies, even more than other vegetables, are an outstanding rich in vitamin C. If you want spicy cuisine, you are here for luck. There are plenty of less "hard" chilies accessible for those averse to intense spicy recipes that can have the same advantages without the burning feeling. Even chilies are improving metabolism. Chilies wellness advantages:

- Chili provides up to 7 times the amount of orange vitamin C, which has a variety of health benefits like combating sinus inflammation, improving metabolism, which relieving migraines and heart, joint and nerve discomfort.
- Chili has traditionally been used to minimize bio-contamination of food and is often considered a possible weight reduction metabolic accelerator.
- It can also play a part in managing leukemia and removing lung cancer.

↓ Beans

They provide a fantastic source of protein, calcium, magnesium, and folic acid. They are flexible too, helping you to prepare loads of Indian dishes. They also go along for other community's cuisines-from Asian to the USA. Beans Benefits:

- Beans are "heart safe" since they produce reduce cholesterol levels of soluble fiber.
- The bulk of beans are around 2 to 3% fat and do not produce cholesterol unless cooked or packed with other products.
- Beans packed with fiber, avoiding acid reflux will foster regularity.
- The daily intake of beans will reduce the likelihood of cardiovascular disease.

Garlic

Not only is garlic savory, but it is also often known for its numerous medicinal powers. It is a key natural source of antimicrobial agents. For garlic's nutritional benefits:

- Garlic produces a Labeled Allicin compound with strong healing uses.
- Frequent application of garlic (in diet or raw) tends to reduce total cholesterol because of Allicin's antioxidant property.
- The exhilarating properties of garlic safeguard the body from free radicals and slow down collagen depletion leading to loss of conductivity in ageing skin.

Spices

Since ancient times Indian spices have become world-renowned. In addition to their amazing flavor and tastes, several spices are good for you too. Haldi or turmeric has soothing powers, helps to lower cholesterol, and avoids blood clots which may contribute to heart attacks. Cardamom improves metabolism while garam masala ingredients comprise various levels of nutrients, thus facilitating digestion as well. Spices Nutritional advantages:

- Many herbs and spices often provide more antioxidants to suppress the disease than vegetables and fruits.
- Cinnamon has a potent anti-diabetic activity and reduces blood sugar levels.
- Turmeric consists of curcumin, a material with significant antioxidant effects
- Ginger has anti-inflammatory action and may relieve nausea.

Paneer

It is a big part of the vegetarian diet, but it is frequently eaten also by non-vegetarians. Paneer is a flexible meal that lends itself well to several various types of dishes. You can also stop the muscle mass-heavy variety produced from whole milk. Home-made breadcrumbs made of milk produce fewer fatty acids and cholesterol and are much better for you. But can also maintain the large amino and calcium concentrations. Paneer Advantages:

- Up to now, maybe popular knowledge, but paneer is a rich source of protein, particularly for vegetarian diets that do not get their meat intake.
- Since paneer is composed of protein, it steadily absorbs energy into the bloodstream, ensuring that it does not induce a spike in one's blood sugar levels, nor does it provide an immediate rise that will soon decrease.
- Besides being high in protein, paneer is a fantastic source of linoleic — a fatty acid that helps to shed weight by growing the mechanism of burning fat in the body.
- Avoids numerous disorders of the body, such as osteoporosis, knee discomfort and dental issues such as rotting of the teeth and gums.

Flour and Rice

White rice is the most widely-eaten grain in India. You can, though, aim to turn to brown rice, since it incorporates more protein, making it a safer option. The switch to whole wheat flour has become more popular. Even for other wheat items like bread, you should suggest doing the same. Health advantages, which Rice and Flour provide:

- Our bodies require insoluble fibers to help them get rid of waste, so if constipation is an issue, rice and flour — particularly brown rice flour — will help alongside nuts, beans and vegetables such as cabbage — all foods that provide most of the fiber.

- ➢ Rice and flour are high in protein, with an advanced rank of B vitamins.
- ➢ Dietary fiber is an integral portion of every diet. Rice contains dietary fiber and helps to transfer waste products via the digestive tract.

✦ Pulses

The Indian diet is incredibly high in grains. The main instances are rice and pasta but note that pulses are an important part of our staple. Luckily, there are so many varieties of pulses accessible that diversity can always be preserved in your diet. Pulses are abundant in nutritious fibers and nutrients A, B, C and E. Even they produce minerals such as calcium and iron. Over everything, they are the primary source of nutrition in a vegetarian diet. Pulses health advantages:

- ➢ The use of more pulses in your eating habits can reduce your risk of heart disease.
- ➢ Pulses are the item with a lot of sugar. The sugar content lists the diet in terms of how it influences blood sugar.
- ➢ Pulses often render the protein a safe and cheap source.

✦ Leafy Vegetables

In the Indian diet, green leafy vegetables already are common. Yet they can be placed to further use. During the whole year Spinach is found throughout the region.

Cabbages are also available in several areas throughout the year, too. Furthermore, hundreds of different types of leafy greens are just ready to include in your diet, depending on where in the world you reside. Leafy Vegetation has health advantages:

- Mustard and Kale greens aid reduce cholesterol.
- Leafy greens maintain good vision and reduce the likelihood of cataracts and improve the clarity you can see.
- They help to feed the body and create electricity.
- They have a mildly acidic taste: It represents their elevated calcium levels.

Eggs Proceed

Although they are not necessarily a choice for vegetarian diets, they are excellent protein sources. The yolk does produce cholesterol – even if you are careful about eating the whole thing, the egg-white will help the body get the necessary minerals and nutrients. You can add eggs to almost every plate. Health advantages that Eggs provide:

- Eggs provide a very great method of free, high-quality protein.
- Feeding small kid's just one egg per day for six months, coupled with a decreased sugar-sweetened diet, can help them reach a healthy height.
- Eggs are rich in cholesterol but do not negatively impact cholesterol throughout the tissue.
- Eggs are high in some nutrients which support cardiac protection.

1.4 Health Benefits of Consuming Indian Food

The use of spices like onion, turmeric, ginger and garlic in the recipe contributes to several health advantages such as better cholesterol, lower risk of cancer and better kidney function. While we know that Indian food has several medical advantages, including spices and vegetables, you may be shocked that Indian food is not always safe. Most Indian cuisine is plant-based. Research shows there are several positive effects of consuming a plant-based diet. Some of these advantages are listed below:

- A healthy Vegetarian Diet

Indian dishes are perfect nutritious recipes, using a wide range of vegetables, legumes, and grains. The mixture of rice that helps you to get full protein. Since Indian ingredients use a variety of foods every day, all the minerals and vitamins found in different plants are more likely to be collected.

There are several nutrients and antioxidants in the vegetables in these dishes that are good for health, liver and brain. The Sulphur compounds present in garlic, cauliflower, and cabbage, for example, help detoxify the body from mycotoxins and toxic toxins.

- Anti-Inflammatory Effect

Turmeric and other spices give anti-inflammatory properties and reduce the likelihood of several chronic disorders. They frequently help relieve inflammation.

Other spices minimize inflammation, improve metabolism, aid weight control and aid detoxify the body. Often, cinnamon tends to control blood sugar levels. If you want your Indian dish to be hot and spicy, the chili is your buddy not just for your taste sense but also for your general health. Chilies are accessed of vitamin C and vitamin A.

- **Higher Concentrations of Fiber**

Good sources of both soluble and insoluble fibers are chickpeas, green vegetables, corn, grains, lentils, green beans etc. When immersed in water, soluble fibers from the peas and beans form a gel-like material. It plays a significant role in reducing your cholesterol levels and regulating your blood sugar levels. Insoluble dietary fiber facilitates regularity in the intestines and avoids indigestion.

- **Ghee Wellness Facilities**

In reality, ghee is nutritious, and if used correctly in balance, it has healing characteristics. Pure cow ghee is a key product in Indian and Ayurvedic medicinal cooking. You will use ghee as an alternative technique to butter, palm oil and hydrolyzed fat on the market. The explanation is because ghee's chemical composition is more robust than olive oil, and it does not quickly flame or get rancid. The concern for much on the market vegetable oil is that the molecular structure starts to break down during the process of heating. They quickly get oxidized and create several complications in the body by growing the number of free radicals. And you actually even know yourself how awful saturated fat is. Clarified butter or ghee, on the other side, helps guard against the toxins and supplies important fatty acids for the hormone development in the body. Ghee decreases inflammation, facilitates nutrition and improves metabolism as per Ayurveda.

1.5 How is Home Cooked Indian Food Different from Restaurant Food?

South Asian cuisine is salty, fatty, wholesome and absolutely delicious cuisine. Indian cuisine is a significant feature of U.S.-Asian life, whether in the warmth of their own homes or at a local restaurant.

Eating out, however, was not a practice among the prior eras of South Asians who were settling in the US. Many saw it as something they did not do back home, an unnecessary privilege, distrusting the recipes or culinary style of 'outside' cuisine, believing the cuisine was designed for the English palate and classifying it as an elite practice. It was the custom to prepare at home, only rarely did US-Asian family go out to dinner. Many stayed as extended families in the same home for up to three families and dining out was not even a choice.

Today, in Indian restaurants, young people of USA-Asians are dining out more, bringing families out for dinner, getting take-outs and not preparing as much at home as in the past. The notion of dining out in Asian Americans is, therefore, a question of preference and culture, not hindered by disparities between generations.

And What Might be better? Home Eating or Out?

Many USA Asians also love home-made food as they feel that it is unique because of the raw vegetables and the freedom to put something you like into your own oven. Others say going out to eat makes a night more fun, sociable and calming. Although all have their positive and bad points, Asians in the USA love a hot curry and enjoy it more when there is a choice to choose from. This is where restaurant cuisine comes in handy, as it offers various meals for all of you who want to eat. So if you are with your mates, you may select from a list and eat whatever you want, but if you are at home, let's just agree it is easier to consume everything.

However, food can always be roasted at restaurants to accommodate the crowd, rather than the person. Chicken Tikka Masala, for example, is a very common restaurant recipe, and maybe never named it in an Asian home when made.

Personalized ingredients are used at home to create such a dish centered on relatives or previously acquired recipes. Ingredients like unique herbs, achaar, or yoghurt are used to create such a recipe that fits your own palate.

Asians enjoy the food but most especially eat it as quickly as possible on our tables. Eating in does not necessarily mean you are going to eat on time, since preparing Asian meals at home will take time utilizing established fresh produce and recipes. It is giving love and attention to your home, always cooking pays-off, particularly if it's something unique for someone!

You have a starter at restaurants, a main dish meal as well as a cake, but this is not that much for those of you with a huge appetite. You can feel like you do not get your money worth as the sizes of the section are rather limited. A Lamb Balti bowl, for instance, can cost around $6-8. If cooking at home, this quantity may suffice for you and your guests, with larger serving sizes and the opportunity, if needed, to incorporate more. All of us, Asians, are now victims to the fast-food community as Britain gets more urbanized. This is because of the hectic lives that we all live through. While most of the old people enjoy a good home-cooked dinner, the new ones consider it more convenient to eat out.

Chapter 02: Common Spices Used in Indian Cuisine and their Properties

Indian food includes the use of a large range of spices. They are mixed and used extensively in different recipes The same spice flavor may be rendered completely different with a slight change in the style of cooking. To discover these amazing products, we have identified several of India's most frequently used spices.

ⵜ Red Powder Chili

Red chili is produced of red chili seeds. It is extremely solid, being the strongest component of the chili, only used in limited amounts. The Americans and the Portuguese brought this substance to India, which has became an important part of Indian cuisine. Even the chili is used in numerous Southern Indian curries. The key feature of chili is hotness, probably due to its capsaicin portion, but there are types that also have a lot of fragrance and flavor.

✦ Mustard Seeds

Brown mustard seeds are more widely used in Indian cuisine than any other mustard seeds. These seeds may be roasted whole for flavoring oil which is then used for cooking raw food. Even this favourite oil may be used as a dipping sauce. Although the seeds are local in Rome, the closest approximation to their usage is in Buddha literature, where he uses certain seeds to save the life of a child.

✦ Coriander

Coriander is a part of the Parsley Genus, and when they mature, the seeds are round, ridged, and change its color from dark green to bright orange. This spice looks tangy and pleasant, with a mild citrusy aroma. This invisible spice is undoubtedly the world's oldest and is commonly cultivated in Rajasthan States.

✦ Cinnamon

Cinnamon is a sweet-flavored spice with a soft and woody fragrance. It is a perfect product for use in sweets and cakes. Cinnamon also has numerous benefits, including bringing spice to the food. Also it helps to reduce leukaemia and lower cholesterol. It is cultivated primarily along the Kerela and Tamil Nadu Western Ghats.

✦ Asafoetida

This is the cured resin emerging from a plant's base. It is particularly pungent in its natural state with a garlic like sulphur scent. However, the scent dies down when cooked in oil, and the flavour significantly improves.

Typically, asafoetida is added to boiling oil before some other component. It is prized for its truffle-like taste and roasted garlic scent and it is used in Indian food as a seasoning blend and flavoring agent. Asafoetida, grown primarily in Kashmir and some parts of Punjab. It is very beneficial for its bashing flatulence properties.

✤ Cumin

Cumin is extracted from the Parsley group and is used in most Indian sauces and veggies to give a smoky flavor and a strong fragrance. Cumin seeds are fried in its dry shape and cooked before use. It is typically the very first spice to be added while preparing Indian foods. It is often roasted dry and reduced to dust before adding to dishes such as pancakes and heavy cream. It is also used for flavoring meat, stuffed onions and tonnes of Indian cooking. It is used carefully since it burns quickly and may become intoxicating.

✤ Saffron

Saffron is the world's costly spice. Actually originated in Kashmir and originating from the prejudice of Cocus Bulbs. It is considered that saffron is more precious than money. Its most notable thing is its musky, honey-like scent. It is commonly used after soaking in water or milk, which eases its intense fragrance and taste.

✤ Tumeric

Another spice that belongs to the ginger tribe is tumeric. It is possibly the spice used mostly in India. Turmeric has been used primarily as a pigment, and for hundreds of years in traditional Ayurvedic. Generated from the roots of the Indian born leafy plant Curcuma Longa.

It has an oaky quality and mild smell and flavour. It is used in items intended for cooking and skincare products. It has a wide variety of medical applications. It aids in coping with skin issues. Its powder could be used to heal open wounds. It also allows to deal with diabetes.

Cardamom

It is the world's third most costly spice, primarily since it needs a lot of physical work. While it has a moderate and soft eucalyptus colour on the green cardamom, the black cardamom is coarse, smoky and usually mostly used for its seeds. The most popular usage for cardamom is to improve tea and pudding taste.

It is used to provide a strong taste and scent in most Indian and other sweet dishes. It is commonly used in the drug industry . It helps protect against poor smell and stomach disease. Whole chewed cardamom is ideal for dealing with diabetes.

Indian Bay Leaf

Indian Bay Leaf is quite distinct from European Bay Leaf even though both belong to the Lauraceae tribe. They are the leaves of a cinnamon tree parent and are distinctive from their white shelves streaks that extend through the root. They are extremely light but have a heavy spice taste.

It grows in northern India, Himalayan slopes and Nepal. Sikkim State is the biggest producer in India, but it is most frequently formed from raw or wild plants. It is a critical element in Mughal food and produced in popular dishes like Korma and biryani.

Ginger

Ginger is one of India's most valuable crops, with more than one thousand tonnes growth per year.

Mostly the fresh ginger is used. Dry ginger is used only in certain states in India, such as Goa and Kashmir.

There are two major ginger types, called after the port they were transported from "Cochin" in the south of Kerala, and "Calicut" in the north of Kerala. Both are strongly aromatic with about 4 percent essential oil content and low fibre content. Owing to its milder and more nuanced taste, it is found to be superior to ginger grown in many other countries. Dried ginger is not as common as fresh ginger in Indian dishes.

⁌ Leaves Curry

The curry leaves, which have little to do with spice, are the leaf of a bush in the Rutaceae family, which is local to India and Sri Lanka. This vegetation is very smelly and friendly. The curry tree is now cultivated in all parts of India but it is more cultivated in the Southern India. So many households have a plant in their greenhouse because it is simple to cultivate. The leaves are often used in the north (for example combined with potato and peas samosa stuffing). They are used in sauces of beef and poultry.

⁌ Kalonji / Nigella

This plant has black triangular seeds, sometimes mistakenly referred to as black cumin, have a mild and somewhat bitter taste, with earthy tones and an onion-like pungent flavour. India is the leading supplier of Kalonji. Egypt and Morocco are the other production countries.

These seeds are also a potent antioxidant and are associated with several medicinal effects, against asthma, fever, pneumonia and other fall diseases.

✤ Ajowan

Another seed spice from a member of the family Umbelliferae is Ajowan. It has a faint bitter earthy flavour, and a fragrance identical to thyme but more strong. The process of cooking (especially baking) smooths the tendency to influence Ajowan, thus producing a rather peculiar nutty taste.

Rajasthan is India's leading Ajowan manufacturer, responsible for 90 percent of total production. Sometimes used for savoury snacks and baked goods in Indian cuisine, it gives a savoury feel to many vegetable meals. Its therapeutic properties vary from assisting with digestion to curing colds and eliminating bloating.

✤ Dark Brown Mustard

It is one of the few seasonings that is as popular in the states having the most flavor consuming nations such as Indonesia and India. In Europe and America, mustard seeds are almost solely used for producing the sauce of the very same name originating from the Roman mixture of mustard seeds with their distinctive sourness.

There are three mustard types that are the light, the brown and the black. The light one is the gentler, whereas the other two are pungent. It is also part of the North-East traditional spice blend. In this area, there is an Indian variant of mustard sauce produced from a mixture of mustard seeds that are soaked for a few days.

Mustard seeds only produce their pungency when grounded or compressed and combined with a fluid using the sourness and stabilise it with an acidic fluid.

✤ Fenugreek

Fenugreek is a herb of the Legumes family. Its plants are used in fresh, dry, and seed forms.

The Hindi word is Methi. Its flavour is whacky and sour (toasting the seeds decreases the bitterness) and its usage is as common as a medicinal treatment in the kitchen. The seeds as a spice are mainly used in India, Turkey, but India is the main source and purchaser of it.

It is an essential component of curry in the kitchen. In Punjab, it is used to complement the flavour of vegetables such as pumpkin, and in the Southern India it is applied to dosa. Batter-dosa includes tasty Indian rice and dal pancakes (split lentils). It is also a component of the Bengali five-spice blend.

According to conventional medicine, it improves absorption and decreases the amount of sugar. It is often used to manage colitis and is recommended for mothers who are breastfeeding since it has a material that enhances the supply of milk.

Clove

This tasty spice is the crisped unlabeled bud of a Myrtle family vine, indigenous to the island chains of Moluccas. The production of cloves extended beyond the Moluccas only towards the end of the XVIII century and the dominance was established. Now mostly in Indonesia, as well as in Tanzania, clove is still produced. South India production began in 1800 but mostly the clove now eaten is transported from Sri Lanka. The usage of clove in Indian cooking is restricted to mixes and masala. It is very high in fragrance and flavour. It is also used in many rice dishes.

Clove has one of the largest proportion of volatile oil relative to other spices, and a tiny quantity goes a long way for this. Clove is also the seasoning with the strongest antioxidant potential.

- **Black Pepper**

Pepper is the spice produced from the Piper nigrum plant berries. We do have three most popular varieties of pepper as per the period of harvest and the post-harvest process: white pepper, black pepper and green pepper.

In India, it is native in the southern area of Malabar and now Black Pepper also grows in Kerala, which is obtained by extracting the green drupes only as they are ripe and begin to turn red, and then by processing them under the sunlight or in a furnace until the humidity content is below a certain level. A process of oxidation occurs during the drying period. Black pepper can be used in many spice mixtures, meat and chicken dishes in the north.

- **Amchur Powder**

This is a sweet and malty spice which acts as a thickening agent and it is used as a dipping sauce. It gives a sour fruity taste to curries, sauces and chutneys.

Chapter 03: Indian Breakfast Recipes

The Indian Breakfast Recipes can be cooked in less time and can be useful for every one of you. Both Northern India breakfast dishes and Southern India breakfast dishes which can be cooked in a matter of minutes, are scattered throughout this chapter. Look at these Indian Recipes for the breakfast and brunch. You will now make them at home in the mornings easily by following given recipes.

↓ Vegetable Rava Upma

Cooking time: 20 minutes

Serving meals: 2

❖ **Ingredients**

- 1 cup of Rava
- 1 sliced onion

- ¼ cup peas
- 1 cup of combined, diced vegetables
- 3 green, sliced chilies
- 1 tablespoon of ginger, sliced
- Just a couple leaves of curry
- ½ teaspoon urad dal
- ¼ teaspoon of mustard seeds
- Leaves of coriander, sliced, to marinade
- Oil 1 tablespoon
- Salt as per your liking

❖ **Method**

1) Take a big saucepan and add vegetable oil and heat it over medium-high heat.
2) Add all seeds that are finely chopped, red chilies and ginger. With a wooden skewer, blend the products together properly.
3) In a pan, add peas and dal in order to combine the products properly, flip the pan tightly.
4) Stir fry for a few moments then add curry leaves. Meanwhile, grab a cutting board and individually cut all the vegetables. Now in the pan put chopped vegetables and mix it all well.
5) Add ample water to the pan and sprinkle very well salt. Use a lid to cover the pan and cook it over medium-high heat.
6) Cook until a deep mixture is created. Now, for a couple of minutes, take a non-stick pan and add 1 tablespoon of oil and cook semolina in it over medium-high heat.

7) When vegetables are fried, add cooked semolina in small amount steadily, stirring constantly. Keep continuously stirring, and check that no chunks are created.
8) Cook on a low flame for 5 minutes and then move it to a serving bowl. Garnish it with cashews and mint leaves.
9) Serve immediately.

Upma Sooji with Coconut

Cooking time: 30 minutes

Servings: 4 persons

❖ **Ingredients**
- 1 cup sooji (semolina)
- 2 teaspoons of ghee
- 1 ½ teaspoon mustard seed
- Asafetida as much you like
- 10 split organic cashews
- 1 teaspoon of Chana dal and urad dal immersed in a bath at least for 10 minutes.
- 1 diced ginger tablespoon
- 1 tiny sliced red onion
- 1 diced green chili
- 10 leaves of curry
- 4 tablespoons of green peas
- 2.5 cups of water
- Salt as much you like
- 2 teaspoons of cilantro minced

- 1 teaspoon of ghee

❖ **Method**

1) Roast the sooji over a moderate flame until moist, continue to stir for around 5 minute. Take sooji off the pan and move it to some other dish.

2) This phase of frying sooji can be completed before and you can save time for packed mornings.

3) Now add two tablespoons of oil at medium heat to the same pan.

4) Then add seeds, hing, cashews, dal ginger and stir fry for 1 minute before they begin to change color.

5) Add carrot, green chili pepper and curry leaves. Once the onions are added, cook for an additional minute.

6) Then after sometime add the peas and stir. Heat till the fresh scent of peas falls out.

7) Add 3 cups of water. Then squeezed lemon zest into it and add cilantro and then, blend properly. If you want a little sweetness in your Upma, you can also add honey or sugar.

8) Put the water in it to a boil now. Until the water has boiled, start adding the cooked sooji little by little at the moment.

9) With a dough scraper, blend sooji in one way after each inclusion.

10) Then cover it with a lid over the pot and adjust heat to normal. Let it stay this way for some time.

11) Remove the cover and add ghee 2 teaspoon. That is voluntary, but it is encouraged. Switch the heat off.

12) Upma is served warm with coconut chutney.

❖ Puffed Upma Rice

Serving to 1–2 persons

Cooking time: 15 minutes

- ❖ **Ingredients**
    - 3 puffed rice cups
    - 1 tiny onion
    - 1 tiny tomato
    - 1-2 chilies
    - ½ teaspoon powder of turmeric
    - Seeds with ½ teaspoon mustard
    - 1 sliced dry red chili
    - Just a couple leaves of curry
    - 2 teaspoon of oil
    - Salt as per your liking
- ❖ **Methods**

1) Chop everything.
2) Heat a skillet with one tablespoon of oil. Add seeds in it.
3) Insert dry red chili and urad dal in the frying seeds. Fry until dal turns into brown color.
4) And add all chopped stuff in it.
5) Also, salt as per your liking and turmeric in it.
6) Cover for a minute and let it cook for a while.

7) Take the puffed rice and add running water via the puffed rice to literally wash it. Try squeezing the water out and quickly return it to the plate.
8) Add it in a pan. And cook over high heat for a moment.
9) Remove it from the heat.
10) Immediately serve puffed Upma rice.

❖ **Things to be Noted**
- Do not wash the puffed rice in water, as it gets soggy.
- Upma-puffed rice is better eaten when wet.

✦ **Tamarind and Rava Upma Rice**

Cooking time: 20-30 min

Serves 6-8 people

❖ **Ingredients**
- 2 cups Rava rice
- 1 onion thinly chopped
- 3-4 green chili with a cut
- ½ roughly chopped ginger
- 1 cup of minced vegetables
- 1 ½ teaspoons ghee
- 9 cashew-nuts (optional)
- 4 cups of water
- Salt

For Seasoning Purposes:
- 1 teaspoon of mustard seeds
- 1 curry sprig leaves

- 1 teaspoon seeds of cumin
- 1 teaspoon gram of Bengal
- 1 teaspoon black dal

❖ **Method**

1) In a pan, heat the oil, add cumin and seeds in it.
2) Insert curry leaves, onion and green chilies and then let the color change with the leaves.
3) Add the dal in it and fry until the dal is finely baked in oil.
4) Add water in it and let it to boil. Put salt as per your liking.
5) Add rice rava constantly when cooking.
6) Stir well, cover the lid and cook over medium-high heat until all of the humidity is consumed.
7) Lower the flame and steam until they are cooked.
8) Turn the heat off and serve it.

✤ **Ragi Rava Idli**

It helps to protect the integrity of the bones and avoids osteoporosis for those with low haemoglobin concentrations. It is a decent source of natural fiber and is gluten free as well. Ragi idli is a really nutritious meal which is ideal for children and the elderly. These idlis are soft, healthy and spongy.

Servings: 4 persons

❖ **Ingredients**

- Idli rice 1 cup
- Flour 2 cups
- 1 cup dal
- ½ teaspoon seeds of fenugreek

- Salt if required

❖ Steps to Follow

1) Wash and soak seeds, urad dal and fenugreek for 4 hours. For 5 hours, clean and rinse the rice independently.

2) Crush dal and seeds until it become sleek and creamy. Remove in a container, and set it aside.

3) Crush the rice to make it flour and add water in it to prepare a visibly rough mixture or batter.

4) Now add rice batter into a dal seeds mixture. Add salt and other spices all together until combined properly.

5) The strength of the batter should be close to the Idli batter.

6) Take the wet blender out of it and blend really well with your fingertips.

7) Allow it to settle for some time. To keep it from spilling, use a wide vessel since it can double during fermentation.

8) Our batter Ragi Idli is set.

❖ How to Cook Ragi Idli

1) Hot the water in an idle or steamer vessel. Mix well the soaked ragi idli batter and pour a spoonful of idli batter in the oiled moulds and put it into the broiler pan.

2) Heat to cook for 20 minutes or a toothpick placed in the idli core comes out clean.

3) After 5 minutes, extract it from the mould using a teaspoon submerged in water.

4) Serve the hot Ragi Idli with your option of chutney.

↓ Rava Idli Sabbakki

Cook Time: 12 minutes

Servings: 15

- ❖ **Ingredients**
  - 1 Sooji cup
  - 1 tablespoon mustard seeds
  - Cumin seeds with one teaspoon
  - 1 tablespoon Chana dal
  - 1 tablespoon Black Dal (Split)
  - Cashew nuts 1/3 cup, sliced
  - 1 sprig of shredded curry leaves
  - Ginger 1 tablespoon
  - Asafoetida as per your liking
  - 2 chilies, chopped
  - Oil as per your use
  - 2 tablespoons of coriander thinly sliced
  - Salt
  - ¼ cup Tapioca Perls
  - 1 cup Curd, battered
  - Oil for greasing

- ❖ **Method**

1) Firstly, simmer tapioca perls in enough water for two hours. Filter this and squeeze out the extra water using your fingertips, do not panic if it partially crumbles or loses its form.

2) In a moderate-flame pan, heat oil. Add seeds and let it vibrate. After some time add cumin seeds and dal mixture. Mix in a low flame until it becomes golden

3) Add hinges, curry, ginger and chilies at this point and cook for 5 minutes, ensure that the products are cooked perfectly.

4) This helps the Rava idli mix to be processed for potential usage in an airtight bag. Add the Rava and roast, then switch off the flame after 5 minutes.

5) Heat water in idli steamer. Lubricate the moulds of Idli.

6) Add Rava idli mixture, strained tapioca perls, coriander leaves, salt as per your liking and yoghurt in a bowl and mix and give it a nice blend.

7) Change the batter's reliability to a thick consistency.

8) Force the batter into the idli mould and heat for 15 minutes.

9) Sprinkle with some oil and serve it.

Rava Idli: Foxtail Millet

Cooking time: 10 minutes

Servings: 3

- **Ingredients**
  - Millet Foxtail-3 cups
  - Dal: 1 cup
  - Fenugreek Seed – ¼ tablespoon
  - Oil as required
  - Water as required
  - Salt as per your liking

❖ **Method**

1) Clean and simmer the millet and Urad Dal in different bowl of water for 6 hours. Along with the Dal, you can immerse Fenugreek seeds in water.

2) Crush your millet and Dal individually.

3) Move the soaked dal and Fenugreek beans in a processor and grind them to a fine paste. Drop it into a bowl. Next, grind the submerged millet in the same blender. Shift it and the Dal batter to the bowl.

4) Balance well the batter and all that for overnight to ferment. Mix well after fermenting.

5) Add salt and blend properly before frying. Add the necessary water to the batter to prepare Idli and get to the consistency of the idli batter. Lubricate the idli plate with butter, then steam for 10 mins in medium-low heat.

6) Enable it to cool down a bit, then sprinkle with little water and extract the hot Idli.

7) Add water to prepare the dosa and change the batter to the consistency required. Heat a dosa tawa and pour a spoonful of batter and distribute evenly. Cook and sprinkle oil around the rim.

8) Flip the other side and fry and then serve it.

✤ **Dosa Rava Onion**

Cooking time: 15 minutes

Servings to 3 persons

- ❖ **Ingredients**
    - Half cup of semolina (sooji)
    - 2 teaspoons sliced coriander
    - 1 sprig Stripped curry
    - Half cup flour of rice
    - 1 tablespoon roughly minced ginger
    - 1 sliced chili
    - ¼ cup of Maida
    - One teaspoon cumin seeds
    - 1 thinly sliced onion
    - Ghee-where appropriate

- ❖ **Method**

1) Get all of the products in a cup except onions and add water. For fast mixing use a whisker.
2) Hold aside the onions. The batter must be really thin.
3) Preferably, heat a non-stick dosa plate. It should be heated. Drizzle and spill the soupy batter with some grease, first making a larger ring and then filling in the middle.
4) Instantly scatter over the sliced onions on it. Add a teaspoon of oil/ghee to it. Let the moderate flame cook till the dosa turns to a golden hue.
5) Then serve it.

⊥ Dosa Buckwheat

It is simple to prepare this nutritious and safe dosa and it is a perfect replacement for bread. Buckwheat has a robust and mildly nutty taste that goes well with a number of fillings.

This recipe allows the batter to rest for at least overnight to enable the flours to be mixed with water. We schedule this and make it stand over time so that the next day it is able to be used. The batter can be kept for up to 2 days in the fridge.

Servings: 10 persons

Cooking time: 10 min

- ❖ **Ingredients**

  - 1 cup of flour for Buckwheat
  - ½ cup Oat flour
  - ½ cup almond flour
  - Water as your liking
  - ½ tsp of salt

- ❖ **Method**

1) To prepare a softer batter: whisk Buckwheat, oat, and salted almond flours. Cover and allow to remain in the refrigerator at room temperature for at overnight.
2) Add water and mix it well.
3) Set a temperature for Dosa maker machine to setting 1.
4) To the upper and bottom cooking racks, grease it with a thin layer of oil. Pour spoonful of batter in.
5) Cook for 3 minutes. Open to inspect the dosa, and cook for 1 minute if necessary.
6) Serve it.

✦ **Dosa Dhania Palak**

Cooking Time 10 min

For 5 Individuals

- ❖ **Ingredients**
  - 2 ½ cups rice, has to be soaked overnight
  - 1 cup Dal, has to be soaked overnight
  - One tablespoon Fenugreek Seeds
  - Salt as per your liking
  - Leaves of Spinach and Coriander, finely sliced
  - Oil to use

- ❖ **Method**

1) For the preparation of dosa, wash the rice, spinach and coriander in water. Let the rice completely submerged in water. Let it simmer for about six hours.

2) Drench the dal and fenugreek in water, so that the whole dal is fully submerged in water. Let them simmer for about six hours.

3) When saturated, grind the dal into a fluffy batter. Only add sufficient water when grinding to turn it into a really softer batter. The batter is going to appear fluffy. Put this batter into a bowl.

4) Crush the rice into a somewhat smooth batter, add only the amount of water needed to process. Using a lot of water would make it too watery for the dosa mixture. The rice batter can be a little bit softer, but it must be extremely soft for the dal batter.

5) Merge the dal and the rice batter, add salt as per your liking and settle it down for the batter fermentation process for at least overnight. You will note that the amount of the batter will have gone up. That is why you can position the batter in a wide jar.

6) In a blender grinder, blend spinach leaves and coriander to create a perfect paste and hold aside.

7) Stir rapidly with a spatula until the batter gets its thickness, and add the salt as per the flavor.

8) Now add the paste and combine the vegetable mixture, so that all is well absorbed.

9) Steam a dosa, and apply a few drops of oil. Lubricate the tawa(pan) with a limited quantity of oil.

10) Take a batter handful and drop back down in the tawa middle. Spread it uniformly in a clockwise direction into the outside.

11) Apply a few drops of oil from the edges and even in the middle. Fry the dosa till it gets brown at the bottom. And then serve it.

+ **Dosa Aval**

Cooking time: 20 mins

Servings to 4 persons

- **Ingredients**
    - 3 cups of rice
    - 1 cup dal
    - 2 tsp fenugreek seeds
    - Salt
    - Ghee or oil, as per your liking
    - Water according to requirements

- **Method**

1) Rinse rice in the water and dal in running water individually, and simmer it in containers with just enough salted water.

2) Let the rice and dal simmer in the bath for a minimum of 6 hours before overnight.
3) Wash aval and add it to the washed rice bowl with water.
4) Grind the dal, rice mixture and fenugreek seeds in a grinder until it becomes smooth batter.
5) Set the oven for 15 minutes to 180 degrees and then switch it off.
6) Hold the overnight batter in an oven.
7) Add salt in the batter the next day.
8) Heat a Dosa Tawa and pour a ladle of dosa batter.
9) Range uniformly with the aid of a slotted spoon. Sprinkle the sides with some oil.
10) Cook until it turns out to be golden.

Dadpe Pohe

Servings to 3 persons

Cooking time 30 minutes

- **Ingredients**
    - 1 ½ cups Small Flattened Rice
    - 1 cup of onion thinly Sliced
    - ¾ Cup coconut grated
    - Powdered Sugar 2 tablespoon
    - Lemon zest 2-3 teaspoons
    - Fresh Peanuts 3 teaspoons
    - Two tablespoon Leaves of Coriander
    - Salt as per your liking or taste
    - Oil 3 teaspoons

- Asafetida ¼ teaspoon

❖ **Method**

1) Mix the finely sliced onions, coconut grated, cinnamon, sugar and lemon zest.
2) Scatter smooth flattened rice in a bowl and mix at the rim.
3) Heat a pan and add cooking oil to it. Insert the fresh peanuts and fried before they shift hue. Remove and set aside.
4) Now add the mustard seeds to the same hot oil and add the asafetida, chopped chilies and leaves of curry. Turn off the flame and add the turmeric powder. Mix it well.
5) Put this mixture over the ready pohe.
6) Offer a quick flip of the whole mix.
7) Shield and hold aside for around 10 to 15 minutes to merge and relax all the tastes.
8) Serve this tasty Dadpae Pohe for brunch or snack at any time.

Pohe Tomato with Peas

Cooking time: 50 mins

Serving to 3 persons

❖ **Ingredients**

- Two teaspoons of olive oil
- 1 Big, minced onion

- 1 Clove of garlic, thinly minced
- 3 Small-sized tomatoes, thinly sliced
- ½ cup of sugar
- One spoonful of new oregano
- 1 of a cup of water or as you required
- One teaspoon of tomato
- 1 Small diced zucchini,
- 1 cup of peas
- Salt

❖ **Method**

1) Refresh to fill poha with only enough water and keep away for 10 minutes.
2) After 10 minutes, absolutely drain the water, release the poha and separate the lumps, if any.
3) Add salt, turmeric powder, lime zest and red chili powder in it.
4) Use a ladle and blend properly.
5) Heat oil in a large frying pan or large base pan.
6) Add the seeds of mustard and cumin.
7) Let them split.
8) Stir-fry light brown on medium-low flame before the onions transform. Add the vegetables and combine well.
9) After some time add the nuts and poha. Cook it for 5 minutes and blend properly.
10) Move to a bowl for serving.
11) Garnish it with coriander and serve right away.

❖ Rotli's Vaghareli

Serving to 2 persons

Cooking time: 30 minutes

❖ Ingredients

- 4 or 5 chapattis left over
- One cup of yoghurt-a good chance to use the extra natural yoghurt in the refrigerator.
- 2 teaspoons of garlic
- 1 spoonful of mustard seeds.
- Two smashed green chilies
- 1 tablespoon of turmeric
- 1 spoonful of cooking oil
- Salt with flavor
- A tiny collection of cilantro
- One lemon tablespoon

❖ Method

1) Break the chappatis into bits.
2) In a saucepan heat the oil. Add the seeds and switch the heat to medium.
3) Add bits of chappati and swirl them in oil.
4) Mix the mustard, turmeric, garlic, chilies in it.
5) Add a cup and a half of water and yoghurt in it and also mix it well.
6) Add the chapattis to this and let it cook in normal heat.
7) Allow the mixture to cook for 5 minutes, then include sugar and lemon in it.

8) To the mixture, add coriander and stir well. They will soak up the liquids while the chapattis cook. If the mixture begins to cling to the bottom of the saucepan, you may need to add more hot water.

9) With a touch of sweet and sour, the flavor of this dish should be mild, so change the taste to your preference. Serve it.

✤ Bengali Vegetable Form Pohe

Cooking time: 40 minutes

❖ Ingredients

For batter you need:

- Maida ½ cup
- ½ semolina cup (sooji)
- 1 tablespoon of sugar
- 1 tablespoon of shredded fennel seeds
- Evaporated milk 350ml
- Oil as per you needs for frying.

For sugar syrup you need:

- 1 Cup of drinking water
- Four green cardamom
- 1 cup of sugar

❖ Method

1) Get all the items specified for a batter in a medium bowl and blend them properly, so that no chunks are there. Add just a little milk if you like it is too dense. Let it rest for some time.

2) Put the ingredients for sugar sauce in a saucepan and cook them together until you have syrup of one string.

3) Hot enough oil in a pan to deep fry.
4) To shape a tiny pancake of 2 diameters, pour a spoon of flour in the liquid.
5) Fry on medium fire. Cook and turn one side over.
6) Suppose all sides turn brown remove with a spatula and indulge in sugar syrup instantly. Leave for 1 minute to full.
7) Remove hot, and serve it.

✢ The Sesame and Beetroot Thepla

Cooking Time: 25 min

Serving to 2 persons

- ❖ **Ingredients**
  - 1 Grated Beetroot
  - ½ cup of Ground wheat
  - ½ cup of besan
  - ½ teaspoon cumin powder
  - ½ Amchur teaspoon
  - ½ teaspoon powder of Garam masala
  - 1 teaspoon mixture of Red Chili
  - Oil as per you need
  - Salt as per your taste

- ❖ **Directions**

1) Add all the herbs, salt and ghee with the diced beetroot.
2) Also add wheat and besan flour and squeeze a soft mixture with water.
3) Take a small portion and shape it into a thepla.

4) Heat up the Tawa and put a thepla on it.
5) Heat it for about a minutes and then turn it and heat about a minute but at the other side.
6) Serve it with curd.

✤ **Dhokla Buckwheat Corn**

Servings to 5 persons

Cooking time: 35 minutes

❖ **Ingredients**

- Two minced Green Chilies
- Chopped 1 Ginger
- ½ teaspoon soda for frying
- 2 teaspoon of fruit salt
- ½ teaspoon Turmeric powder
- 2 tablespoons Sunflower Oil
- 1/3 cup of Water
- 2 cups Gram (besan) flour
- 1 cup water, or more where possible
- 2 teaspoons of salt to taste

❖ **Method**

1) Start preparing all the items to start cooking the Dhokla.
2) Grease and leave aside a cake tray or a dhokla plate. Get a steamer prepared with water and have it loaded.
3) Next, create a combination of chili and ginger. Add this combination and water into a shallow blender mixer jar and combine to create a puree. Hold this away.

4) Put all the items along with the above paste into a large bowl and hold aside.

5) Whisk well to mix, add lemon zest and soda will froth up the Dhokla batter.

6) Into the lubricated plate, put the Dhokla batter and put it in the steamer ready.

7) Wrap the steamer and switch the heat on and steam it for 15 minutes.

8) If you stick a knife in the middle and along the sides and it falls out dry, you will recognize when it is finished.

9) Remove from the steamer the Khaman Dhokla, and leave it to cool fully.

The next move is to prepare the water in the sugar lemon:

10) Heat a skillet over medium heat with oil. Add the mustard seeds and cumin seeds, and let it crack. Apply the green chilies and curry leaves and mix for about a minute until it crackles.

11) If done, add the water, lemon zest, salt and sugar. Remove it before the sugar dissolves, then switch off the fire. Let the tadka cool off a little.

12) From over Khaman Dhokla, sponge the tadka so that it gets well saturated.

13) Remove it from the pan and serve it.

✢ Paneer Crepes and Green Peas

Cooking time: 45 minutes

Servings to 4 persons

- ❖ **Ingredients**
  - 1 cup Green peas
  - 2 cup of Paneer (Homemade Cheese Cottage)
  - Chopped two tablespoon Ginger
  - 2 Green Chili, sliced
  - 2 teaspoon Turmeric powder
  - 4 teaspoons of Powder Red Chili
  - 2 Amchur teaspoon
  - 2 teaspoon of Powdered Coriander
  - 1 cup wheat flour
  - For kneading, olive oil

- ❖ **Method**

1) Put the sifted flour in a broad mixing cup. Add water a few times to make a moist to the fluffy dough by kneading.

2) When all the dough has become round, drizzle the top of the dough with a teaspoon of oil and knead for another few minutes. Wrap the dough, but we are going to prepare the filling.

3) Heat a skillet with some oil over medium flame. Add cumin seeds in it and allow it to splutter for a couple of seconds. Add all spices, and cook it well. Add peas in it. Cook them until they are half done.

4) Add crushed paneer and cook them well over medium heat before the raw flavor of the spice fades. Hold it to cool away.

5) Divide parts of the dough into medium sized lemon balls.

6) Pat the dough section and sprinkle it with flour. Roll the dough out into a coil 5 inches in diameter. In the middle of the dough, spoon a good part of the filling.

7) Wrap the ends by pulling the ends close. Lightly brush the paratha back into the flour and roll gently to clear any pockets of air.

8) Roll the paratha such that the filling remains within and therefore does not seep out, creating very little strain.

9) The next move is to cook the paratha. Heat up the skillet and put the paratha on it.

10) Switch and cook from both surfaces before external brown stains emerge. Drizzle the paratha with ghee or oil and cook at low to medium heat until both sides have the paratha cooked through it and golden brown.

11) Move the paratha to a plate until finished, and prepare the rest of the Paneer and Green Peas Packed Parathas the same way.

12) Serve it.

✢ Oats Cheela with Paneer Stuffed Palak

Cooking time: 40 minutes

Serving to 4 persons

- ❖ **Ingredients**
    - 1 cup of gram flour
    - Oil from 2 to 3 teaspoon
    - Ginger-1 teaspoon paste
    - Seeds for the carom ¼ teaspoon
    - Chilly red powder- ¼ teaspoon
    - Spinach-1 cup (cut thinly)

- Salt as per you need

❖ **Method**

1) First of all, make a batter again with the besan chilla and take a spoonful of batter.
2) Pour batter over hot Tawa.
3) Spread carefully to ensure a moderately dense chilla.
4) A teaspoon of oil is scattered across the edges.
5) Enable cooking for a minute on low to medium flame, or until the underside is completely cooked.
6) Now softly turn over the chilla without splitting.
7) Make sure all sides of the chilla are prepared.
8) Now spread out part of the chilla with 2 teaspoon of cooked paneer stuffing.
9) Serve it.

Chapter 04: Indian Lunch and Dinner Recipes

The main course meals are taken for lunch and dinner. We may have a light dinner, too, but you can still have a nice breakfast and a better lunch. A list of such recipes has been shared in this chapter which can be served for lunch or dinner. The purpose is not only to share the recipes, but you can also get the collection-based ideas and can seek or make any other dishes not listed here.

⁜ Madras Curry Chicken

Serves to 4 persons

Time to cook: 2 hours

- ❖ **Ingredients**
  - Ghee
  - Onion
  - Coriander
  - Garlic
  - Clean ginger
  - Salt as per your taste
  - Boneless chicken thighs without skin
  - Citrus zest
  - Finely sliced tomatoes
  - Curry Powder
  - Coconut milk

- ❖ **Steps to Follow**

1) Firstly, over medium heat, set up a big pot. Add the sliced onion, chopped garlic, and smashed ginger to the oil. Stir for 10 minutes until the onions become very tender.

2) Then include curry powder, salt and chili powder. Mix and cook it all for some time until it becomes aromatic.

3) Boost the flame to normal, and add the coconut milk and tomatoes in it. Cook it for some time.

4) Then mix the sliced pieces of chicken into the gravy — cover and cook. Frequently stir, for 25 minutes.

5) Finally, in order to finish the sauce, add chopped coriander in it. Just before eating, sprinkle the lemon zest for garnishing.

⚜ Casserole Chicken Tikka Masala

Serving to 4 persons

Cooking time: 3 hours

❖ Ingredients

- Eight chicken bone-in thighs
- 1 tablespoon lime zest

For a marinate

- Ginger-pieces, mashed
- Ten cloves of garlic, mashed
- Yoghurt as per your need
- Chili powder- a pinch
- 1 teaspoon of coriander
- 1 teaspoon cumin
- 1 teaspoon masala garam
- 1 teaspoon of turmeric
- 1 tiny chili

For of the sauce

- 1 ½ tablespoon butter
- 1 big, coarsely diced onion
- 1 tablespoon of cumin seeds
- 1 tablespoon mustard
- ½ teaspoon fenugreek crushed
- ½ teaspoon of paprika
- 3 of cardamom
- 1 big slice of cinnamon

- 1 tablespoon of purée tomato
- 40 g of almonds, chopped
- 1 teaspoon of vinegar
- Milk as per your need.
- Passata as you per your need.

❖ Steps to Follow

1) Cut the chicken skin and slice single thigh 2 to 3 times. Put the chicken pieces, lemon juice and salt in a plastic jar and mix it well. Leave aside while the seasoning is being made.

2) Grind the ginger and garlic in a tiny spice grinder to produce a sauce, add a drop of water if necessary. For the gravy, cast aside a quarter of the paste. In the spice grinder, add the necessary marinade components, then grind to a fine paste.

3) Load the mixture over the chicken in a jar and let it marinate for minimum of 4 hours.

4) On medium flame, heat 2 tablespoons of the ghee in a deep pan to render the sauce. Cook the onions over medium heat for 20 minutes before they start browning.

5) Add the spices and the remaining paste of garlic and ginger, and cook for 5 minutes. Add a sauce of tomatoes, almonds and vinegar in it. Heat it for some time.

6) Put in the passata, then refill the container with water up high. Put it to a moderate flame, then boil for 2-3 hours until a deep sauce is present. It can be kept frozen in the refrigerator for 24 hours while the chicken is marinated.

7) Set the barbecue to its full level.

8) Take a chicken and arrange it on a big, cut-side-up baking sheet. Set 10-15 mins under the grill before charred and start blackening. Take the sheet from the oven.

9) Reheat the sauce, apply the retained marinate and curry sauce in the chicken. Cook until the chicken is fully ready. Leave the curry to stay for a few minutes.

10) Garnish it with cilantro and almonds, then serve it.

✦ Beef Kofta with Saag Aloo

Serves to 4 persons

Cooking time: 1 hour

❖ Ingredients

- 1 onion
- 1 garlic
- 2 small-medium potatoes
- ½ pile of coriander
- ½ teaspoon cumin
- ½ teaspoon turmeric
- ½ teaspoon mustard
- 1 pot of chicken reserve
- 300 g of minced beef
- Coconut Milk as per your need
- ½ teaspoon of lemon zest
- Water

❖ **Steps to Follow**

1) Firstly, cut and slice into bits of onion. Slice the garlic and grind it. Slice the potato into cubes. Cut the coriander loosely.

2) On moderate fire, heat oil in a big frying pan. Add the garlic and onion in it and cook for 5 mins or until it becomes tender. Keep half of this substance out and put it away in a tray.

3) Put the rest onion in the frying pan with the cumin, turmeric, and mustard and mix and cook it for 3 minutes.

4) Add the potato cubes and water as per your need and half a pot of chicken supply. Mix it so that it will dissolve. Cover with a lid, switch the heat to low and boil for around 15-20 mins.

5) In the meanwhile, place the beef in a bowl and mix with salt as per your taste, a decent black pepper and grind.

6) Form the mixture of beef into four small balls per individual. In a frying pan, heat oil on moderate flame and fry until golden brown everywhere.

7) Remove the koftas from the pan.

8) Put the koftas in boiling mixture and boil gently.

9) Add the spinach, then remove the pan from the flame, place the lid on, and keep on the side for 10 minutes. Mix it in the spinach. Put over a little lemon zest and stir it straight. Serve it.

✢ **Chicken Curry Mango**

Serves to 4 persons

Cooking time: 2 hours

❖ **Ingredients**
- 2 teaspoons of coconut oil
- 1 large sliced onion
- 4 cloves of garlic
- 8 teaspoons of chopped ginger
- 4 teaspoons of curry powder
- Salt and pepper, as per your taste
- 3 sliced, diced and split mangos
- Coconut milk as per your need
- 2-4 Chicken thighs, sliced

❖ **Steps to Follow**

1) Heat the coconut oil over a moderate flame in a wide and deep fryer. Add the onion, garlic, and ginger and cook it until they turn out to be brown.

2) Then add the curry powder, salt, pepper, 1 cup of the fresh mangoes, and the coconut milk to the bowl and mix it well.

3) Then add the above sauce to the frying pan and put the chicken and ½ cup of water in it. Cover with a lid and let it cook for 20 minutes. Turn the heat down if the edge of the frying pan starts to cling to the sauce.

4) Add the leftover mango to the plate when the chicken parts are completely cooked and eat.

✢ **Tandoori Curry Sandwich**

Serves to 4 persons

Cooking time: 1 hour

- ❖ Ingredients
  - 1 entire chicken, cut into pieces.
  - 1 cup Greek simple yoghurt
  - ½ yellow, diced onion
  - 1 peeled, freshly grated ginger
  - 2 Garlic Cloves
  - 2 tablespoons healthy citrus juice
  - ½ teaspoon of cumin
  - ½ teaspoon of ground cilantro
  - 1 tablespoon olive oil
  - Salt and potatoes

For making Sandwiches
  - big, half warmed, entire wheat bread
  - Regular Greek yoghurt
  - ½ teaspoon of cumin field
  - ½ teaspoon of ground cilantro
  - ¼ teaspoon garlic powder
  - Salt and tomatoes
  - Lettuce

- ❖ Steps to Follow
1) Put chicken pieces in a big zip-lock bag.
2) Mix milk, onion, ginger, garlic, lemon juice, cumin, coriander, and oil in a food processor, until it becomes creamy. Season with salt and pepper as per your taste.

3) Put the sauce with the chicken into the zip-lock bag and shake to cover it. Just let the chicken marinate in the fridge for a minimum of 4 hours.

4) Preheat the oven up to 500 degrees. Put the chicken into the rack, skin downside. Roast, approximately 35 minutes, before burnt spots begin to emerge on the bird, tossing once. Reduce heat to 450 and proceed to cook, about 10 minutes more, before the chicken is cooked completely.

5) Dice the remaining chicken into pieces of bite-size if you wanted.

6) In a shallow bowl, mix yoghurt and spices. Open each half of the pita to shape a pocket and fill with meat, lettuce, tomato sauce and yoghurt.

✢ Veggie Filled Butter Curry Chicken

Serves to 3 persons

Cooking time 2 hours

- ❖ **Ingredients**
  - Two tablespoons butter
  - One huge white onion, tiny dice
  - 2 big garlic cloves
  - One teaspoon clean ginger
  - One tablespoon Garam Masala
  - One tablespoon curry powder
  - One tablespoon cilantro powder
  - ½ teaspoon paprika
  - ¼ tablespoon cinnamon
  - Chili flakes about ¼ tablespoon

- Two tomatoes
- 1 400 ml coconut milk bottle

❖ **Steps to Follow**

1) Heat coconut oil or butter in a wide skillet or pot over moderate-low heat until it is melted. Add onion in it and cook for around 6 minutes or until it is translucent.

2) Garlic and ginger are added and sautéed for 5 minutes until it turns out to be aromatic, then add garam masala, curry powder, cilantro, paprika and cinnamon. Let it cook for around 1 minute, thus swirling periodically.

3) Add the chili flakes and tomatoes to the jar. For around 15 minutes, let all the sauce boil until the sauce thickness increases and it will become a strong and dark red-brown shade.

4) Remove it from flame and put it into a mixer and add salt as per your taste. Then add up to quarter a cup of water in it if the mixture is too heavy to incorporate. Blend in batches if you have a small blender.

5) Put back the sauce into the tub. Add coconut milk and sugar in it. You would insert your cooked lentils, tomatoes, chickpeas and vegan chicken at this stage and cook it for 10-15 minutes.

6) Represent it with corn and coriander.

✢ **Paneer Pulao**

Serves to 4 persons

Cooking time: 2 hours

❖ **Ingredients**

- One cup of Rice Basmati
- One and half of Paneer cubes

- Half cup of Peas & carrot
- One large Onion
- 2 Green Chilies
- One teaspoon Ginger Garlic Paste
- Leaves of coriander, diced-as desired
- Salt-As required
- Oil or Ghee

❖ **Steps to Follow**

1) For about 30 mins, rinse and soak the rice. On moderate flame, put ghee in a saucepan and let it heat for 3 minutes. Add soaked rice well-drained in it and cook for a while until it becomes dry.

2) Add oil in a pan over moderate flame. Add onion, green chili and fry until the onion is only translucent, without altering its hue.

3) Add the paste of ginger and garlic, fried it and then add the vegetables. Fry them to half-finished vegetables.

4) Add 1 cup water and salt in it and let it cook. Add the rice which is already cooked. Cover with a lid, and cook in moderate flame.

5) Prepare the paneer cubes. For better taste, let the paneer cubes be small. Paneer cubes (previously thawed or immersed in hot water) are typically toasted in a non-stick skillet until it turns out to be golden.

6) Once the pulao is accomplished, the paneer is drained and added to the pulao. Before adding, ensure the water is depleted from the paneer.

✦ Makhni Dal

Serves to 4 persons

Cooking time: 2 hours

❖ Ingredients

- 2 teaspoons of red beans drenched overnight
- 1 spoonful of red chili powder
- 8 teaspoons of butter
- 1 tall, chopped onion
- Half cup of puree tomato
- One-half cup new milk
- Half teaspoon of paste with ginger
- Salt as needed
- Sliced two ginger
- 2 large diced chili
- ½ cup of dal, immersed in water whole night
- Garlic paste of 1/2 teaspoon

❖ Steps to Follow

1) Soak dal overnight in two cups of water. Drain it, then cook in pressure cooker with salt and 3 cups of water. This allows the dal and rajma to become tender.

2) Put a pan on a moderate heat and add the cumin seeds in it. You should slowly add the ginger and garlic paste until the cumin seeds rasp and swirl after some time. You should then add some carrots, sliced green chilies and puree of tomatoes.

3) Fry before it becomes golden mixture. If you are somebody who enjoys Dal Makhani's authentic look, then we recommend that you use ghee rather than oil.

4) When the masala is fit to your liking, you can add the Rajma and dal in it and let it to steam.

5) Then, as per your preference, add garam masala and salt. Carry to a cook and stir well, if you think the dal is too dense, you may add more water.

6) Then add some fresh cream in it and combine well. That will render your creamy and tasty Dal Makhani.

Chicken Lemon

Serves to 4 persons

Cooking time: 2 hours

- ❖ **Ingredients**
  - Four chicken breasts that are skinned
  - One tablespoon of lemon zest
  - 1 tablespoon of honey
  - 1 cup oil
  - 2 cloves of garlic, minced
  - 1 teaspoon of oregano crushed
  - Fresh, green salad and potatoes to eat

- ❖ **Steps to Follow**

1) Warm the gas furnace to 170C. In a deep oven tray, place the chicken into a layer.

2) Add all the available ingredients in a pan and heat it for 1 min in the oven or tiny skillet. Remove all together, then spill over the chicken.

3) Grill the chicken for 45 minutes and roast every 10 minutes. Progressively, the juice thickens to offer the chicken a glossy covering.
4) Allow the chicken to rest for 5 minutes before adding with a green salad and fresh potatoes.

✠ Fry Chittenad Trout

Serves to 2 persons

Cooking time: 2 hours

- ❖ **Ingredients**
  - Fish 400g
  - Powder with turmeric-1 tablespoon
  - Salt as per preference
  - Lemon juice one tablespoon
  - 3 onions
  - 2 Garlic cloves
  - 2 tablespoons of ginger
  - 2 teaspoons of Cumin seeds
  - 2 teaspoons of rice flour
  - Oil as per your need
  - 1 tablespoon of red chili powder
  - Coriander powder -1 tablespoon

- ❖ **Steps to Follow**

1) Carve the fish into bits and wash them with water.
2) Add some turmeric powder, salt, one lemon juice and cover the cod, then set aside.

3) Time to take the blender jar and add the cumin seeds, garlic, ginger and onion in it. And blend to make a paste.
4) To create a dense paste, move the masala paste to a pan and add the red chili powder, coriander powder, and rice flour, salt and add two tablespoons of oil.
5) Remove parts of fish now and cover the masala with even paste on the fish.
6) Let the fish marinate for 2 hours.
7) Then, Heat oil on a grill pan or skillet.
8) When the oil is hot sufficient, add the pieces of fish one by one and fry until they are cooked on one side and then turn to the next hand.
9) Switch the fish to a clean cloth until finished to extract excess fat.
10) Serve it with a cup of freshly boiled rice.

Mutton Do Pyaaza

Serves to 2 persons

Cooking time: 1 hour

❖ Ingredients

- A half kilogram of Mutton
- Half cup of yogurt
- 3 Cardamom
- 5 Chilies or as per your taste
- Half teaspoon of Cinnamon powder
- Half teaspoon of cumin
- 1 tablespoon of garlic pulp
- Salt for flavor

- 1 teaspoon of powdered red chili
- ½ tablespoon of turmeric
- Half cup of Oil
- 3 diced onion
- One teaspoon poppy seeds
- One teaspoon Coconut soil

❖ **Steps to Follow**

1) Clean the beef and hold the strainer in place.
2) Mix yoghurt, cardamom, cinnamon powder, chilies, cumin, a paste of garlic, salt, powder of red chili and turmeric.
3) Add this mixture to the meat and let it rest for 1 hour.
4) In a skillet, heat the oil and fry the onion until it is lightly brown in color. Remove onion in a pan and cook the meat in the same pan.
5) When water from yoghurt dries out, substitute enough liquid to prepare the beef. Cover until tender and cook.
6) Mix in coconut and poppy seeds.
7) Add the fried onion and cook for 2 minutes. And serve it.

✤ **Makhmali Kofte**

Serves to 3 persons

Cooking time: 2 hours

❖ **Ingredients**

For the preparation of the Koftas:

- 400g. Indian Cottage Cheese (Paneer), sliced

- 2 big, baked and mashed potatoes
- 2 chopped Green Chilies
- ¼ teaspoon of white pepper powder
- Two broad tablespoons of corn flour
- 4 tablespoons of oil to prepare
- Salt, for taste

For the preparation of the gravy:

- A quarter cup of oil
- 2 moderate sliced onions
- 1 tablespoon of ginger
- Half a garlic plant, sliced
- 20 cashews, 10 minutes immersed in water
- 1 cup puree tomatoes
- 1 cardamom dark
- 3 Cardamom Gray
- 1 Bay leaf
- 1 pinch of cinnamon
- Half teaspoon of powder chili
- 2 teaspoons of milk
- One teaspoon Kasuri methi also called fenugreek.
- Salt, for taste

❖ **Steps to Follow**

1) Combine all the ingredients well and form them into balls (excluding the oil).

2) In a deep pan, heat the oil and cook the Koftas until both sides are golden brown.

3) Keep half of the chopped onion

4) In a hot oil, fried them until it turns out to be nicely brown.

5) In a processor, mix the leftover onions, ginger, garlic and cashews and blend them into a fine paste.

6) In a shallow pan, heat the oil and add all of the garam masala, black and green cardamom, garlic, bay leaf and cinnamon.

7) Add the paste as the spices shift color. Heat up on the high heat for 3 minutes

8) Add the fried onion and stir fry for 5 minutes.

9) Place in a puree of tomato, red Kashmiri chili and salt. Add a glass of water and cook on a moderate flame for 20 minutes.

10) Gently add the cream and methi when the mixture cools down a little.

11) Pour the sauce into a bowl that is big and deep. One by one, lower the koftas in the sauce, taking caution not to layer them on top of one another.

12) Apply a little cream sprinkling over the end. Serve mild.

- **Pasta Masala**

Serves to 3 persons

Cooking time 1 hour

- ❖ **Ingredients**
  - 1 cup of pasta to pick as per your liking
  - 1 tablespoon of olive oil

- 1 teaspoon of seed cumin
- 3 sliced garlic cloves
- 1 tiny sliced onion
- 3 thin, diced tomatoes
- 1 tablespoon powder of turmeric
- 1 teaspoon of option curry powder
- 1 tablespoon powder of coriander
- Ground red chili as per your taste
- Salt as per your taste
- 1 cup of water or, as needed

❖ **Step to Follow**

1) Place an electric pot in high stir fry mode. Add oil, then let it get warm.
2) Add garlic, onions and cumin seed and cook for a while.
3) Now add the tomatoes and cook them until they are tender. Include all the dried spices and salt.
4) Fry for one or two minutes.
5) Add pasta and water. Mix properly, then turn off stir fry mode.
6) Set it to mode high for 7 minutes, holding the ventilation to sealing spot. After 10 minutes, unlock it.
7) Serve it as per your liking.

✦ **Garlic Mushrooms**

Serves to 3 persons

Cooking time: 1 hour

❖ **Ingredients**
- 2 tablespoons of butter
- Oil: 2 tablespoons
- Quarter cup of finely sliced onion
- 1 cup of Mushrooms Button
- 2 tablespoons of finely ground garlic
- 2 tablespoons Parsley Fresh, Split, thinly sliced
- ½ teaspoon thyme, finely minced
- Oregano New, ½ tablespoon, Finely chopped
- Red chili flakes as per your taste

❖ **Steps to Follow**
1) In a non-stick skillet, add oil and butter and cook over low or moderate heat.
2) Add onions in it and stir fry for 3 minutes.
3) Include the mushrooms and fry until it turns out to be light brown.
4) Add all the spices and stir and cook it well.
5) Cook until it is flavor-some with garlic. Be alert not to let the garlic burn.
6) Add the rest parsley and turn off the heat easily and enjoy it.

Chapter 05: Indian Dessert Recipes

Dessert is the icing on a plate. There is no doubt saying that desserts offer every meal a satisfactory ending. No wonder, people have a weakness for sweets and deserts. Not only are deserts part of our staple food, but they are also even served in many worship areas. By and wide, sugar, milk and khoya are used as staple ingredients in all Indian desserts.

- Shahi Falooda
- Ingredients
    - Two bottles of milk
    - 2 tablespoon of rice
    - Two tablespoons of Honey
    - Two teaspoons of syrup of flavor

- Two tablespoons of dry fruits as per your choice and preference, minced finely

❖ **Steps to Follow**

1) Cook the rice in water for 15 minutes or so — strain to cool it down and set it aside.
2) In a mixer, add the milk, sugar, and dry fruit and blend until it turns out to be creamy.
3) Place two glasses and put the rice in each of them.
4) Add half of the milk now in them. Blend it well each of them after putting syrup in it and then, cool in the fridge.
5) If you like to use ice cream, add an ice cream scoop to this and seasoning with dried berries. Attach a long-handled serve.

✢ **Gulab Jamun**

❖ **Ingredients**

For the balls of dough:

- 1 cup of condensed milk
- Plain flour 110 g
- One and half of teaspoon of baking powder
- Half teaspoon of soda
- One and a half cup of milk
- 25g of sugar, warmed
- Oil for frying

For the preparation of a syrup:

- 1 cup of caster sugar
- Water 100ml

- Saffron as per your preference

For garnishing:
- 1 tablespoon pistachio nuts sliced
- 1 tablespoon of almonds, toasted in a skillet

❖ **Steps to follow**

1) Blend all the components together in any bowl for the dough balls, adding sufficiently extra water to shape a smooth, sticky dough. Cover and put aside for 20 minutes. Form the dough into tiny, round pieces.

2) Heat oil in a deep fryer with thick sides. Fry the balls thoroughly in it until they turn out to be light brown, then scrape the oil with a serving dish and put aside to drain.

3) Prepare a sugar syrup by boiling the sugar and water along with the saffron.

4) When the balls of dough are cooked, add to the sugar fluid and enable to soak for around 1 hour.

5) Garnish it with nuts and almonds and serve it.

✦ **Kulfi**

❖ **Ingredients**
- 1 liter of whole milk
- Half cup of heavy cream
- 1/3 cup of crushed khoya
- 1 tablespoon dry milk powder, for the flavor
- 3 tablespoons of a combination of cashews and pistachios
- 10 teaspoons of sugar

- Skin separated & smashed by five green cardamom

❖ Steps to follow

1) Add entire milk to a heavy middle pan and put it over low or medium flame.
2) Add cream to it after around 10 minutes, as it heats up a bit.
3) Let the solution simmer and then let the heat down to low.
4) Let the milk boil for around 25 minutes at low heat, constantly stir it in between.
5) The milk will look very thick after about 25-30 minutes, then add crushed khoya and blend at this point. Keep stirring this; it will take 10 minutes to melt the khoya.
6) If the khoya has melted, add the sugar in it and cook until it melts.
7) And also add the nuts which were chopped before. The finely chopped nuts offer more texture to the kulfi.
8) Add the condensed milk and mix. Boil for an extra 5 minutes. At the end of it, it should get very thick, and it will begin to thicken as it cools off.
9) Remove the pan from heat and add cardamom powder in the pan and mix it well. Let it cool off.
10) Until the milk has completely cooled, pour it into kulfi moulds or some other jar of your liking. Cover and freeze it until fully developed.
11) Place the kulfi mould under warm, clean water once it has been frozen and then tap the mould on the counter. The kulfi will quickly fall out. Enjoy the tasty Kulfi malai.

Mishti Doi

Ingredients

- 1 liter of cream milk
- 8 Cardamom
- Curd as per your taste
- 1 cup of sugar or as per your taste

Steps to Follow

1) Heat one liter of cream milk in a deep non-stick saucepan.
2) Stir it continuously while heating the milk.
3) Add a cup of sugar and mix well.
4) Boil the milk over a moderate flame until it becomes dense. Stir periodically, until the milk becomes half of the amount. Meanwhile, put two tablespoon brown sugar in a saucepan. Add the water in it, then blend properly. Stir until the sugar melts, holding fire on low.
5) Transferring caramel sugar to boiling milk.
6) Stir well enough and carry the milk to the next simmer. Now let it cool to the maximum. Move to a clay pot or other jar after the milk is chilled and still slightly wet.
7) Place a teaspoon of curd in and combine well.
8) Shield and allow it to settle for 8 hours in a warm position or until it is completely set.
9) To get a good creamy texture, refrigerate for 2 hours. Sweeten it with sliced nuts as well.
10) Finally, serve chilled mishti doi.

Indian Cham Cham Desert

❖ Ingredients

- Four cups of cream milk
- Paneer as you have prepared this earlier or you take it readymade
- Two cups sugar
- 5 cups of water
- 1/8 tsp powder of cardamom

❖ Steps to Follow

1) Prepare paneer first. Take a small piece of paneer in your hand and rub with your fingertips to verify whether adequate water has been extracted from the paneer or not. After 30 seconds of pressing, to create a strong yet smooth surface.

2) Put the soaked paneer on a flat, smooth edge and knead until it forms into a smooth, soft dough for 3 to 4 minutes. Fill in a teaspoon of water if the paneer is too mushy.

3) Divide the dough of the paneer into eight equal portions and form each into a flat oval face disc.

4) For the syrup: Put 5 cups of water in a large saucepan to boil. Add sugar, then whisk to completely dissolve. Using a wide pan as the Chum Chum doubles in volume as they cook in the syrup.

5) Add the balls of the paneer to the syrup and stir to combine again. Then lower the flame to a medium level and cover with foil. Cook 15 minutes.

6) Open the cover of the pan, turn over the chum chums and cook for a further 15 minutes. Check to see how

the chum chums look solid yet sponge-like. Switch the flame off and leave it to stay for a full 10 minutes.

7) Keep the chum chums off the water. Represent it after chilling.

- **Sitaphal**
- **Ingredients**
    - 1 cup of fresh custard apple pulp (eliminated seeds)
    - 2 White Eggs
    - Cream milk 400 ml, cooled
    - 1/3 cup powdered sugar
    - 1/3 teaspoon of Vanilla extract
- **Steps to Follow**

1) Using a blade, grind the custard apple to a gritty pulp in a large dish.

2) While the Sitaphal is freezing, take a dry container stir the two egg whites in it until they get fuzzy and soft tips are produced in them with a hand beater. The trick is to carefully distinguish the egg white. And the slightest amount of yolk stops the whites from being soft.

3) Mix together all the water, butter, and extract into a small dish. Do not whisk as hard as the cream will transform to butter.

4) Now add the pulp of the custard apple to the milk mixture and blend the two together with a spoon.

5) Add this combination carefully into the egg whites. The aim is to hold as many of the air as possible in the egg whites to get silky, smooth, delicious ice cream. When thoroughly prepared, place in a freezer bowl.

6) Freeze to stand for 3 hours. Erase and stir again from the refrigerator until it becomes smooth.//
7) Put it back in the fridge and keep it again. Scroll out into and feed single pots.

↓ Till Ladu Classical

❖ Ingredients

- 500 gram of flour
- 1 liter of milk or drink
- 750 gram ghee
- 750 grams sugar
- 3 cups of water
- 5-10 drops Color Orange
- 10 to 12 flakes of Saffron, saturated
- 50 cashew, sliced
- Raisins as per you need
- 12 Cardamoms

❖ Steps to Follow

1) Prepare a thin mixture of water and gram flour or milk. Heat ghee in a saucepan.
2) Fill the frying pan or strainer with up to half the batter.
3) Place it in hot ghee over the pan and drain boondis by striking the strainer on the side of the tub, picking up and hitting again. The phase should be done quite easily.
4) Fry them to the color of gold. Using the batter all around.
5) By heating sugar and water, prepare sugar syrup with a one and a half threaded thickness.

6) Add saffron water and color in the syrup. Add the boondis, cardamom, dried fruits and honey. And mix it well.

7) Sprinkle on a little hot water after 10 minutes, cover and retain for 1 ½ hours.

8) Make it in circular spheres by using wet hands.

The Peanut Indian Brittle

❖ **Ingredients**

- One cup-roasted peanut (skin free).
- One cup-of sugar.

❖ **Steps to Follow**

1) Place the peanuts in the blender and grind them into a smooth paste. On a moderate flame, put a pan with the sugar and 2 spoons of water in it. Continue stirring. The sugar transforms steadily into the caramel.

2) As all the lumps melt, turn the heat off, add the peanut powder, blend it properly, shift the paste easily onto a grated tray and spread uniformly.

3) Draw lines with a knife when the paste is hot and allow it to chill.

4) When chilled, divide to create squares along with the outlines.

Indian Barfi

❖ **Ingredients**

- 2 cups of granules of creamy milk
- Hard cream about 300ml
- 400 g Condensed milk that can be sweetened
- Half cup of pistachios finely sliced

❖ **Steps to Follow**

1) Collect all the ingredients.
2) Mix together all milk and cream and whisk it until creamy.
3) Cover the pan and put it in the microwave and set the time for about 8 minutes.
4) Carefully monitor the dish, and if the solution seems like it could boil over, avoid automatically by stopping microwave for 8 to 10 seconds. Start again and work until the duration of 8 minutes has elapsed. Take it out and mix it well.
5) Return the pan to the microwave and put it high again for 8 minutes. Monitor the first minute carefully and then allow the cooking to begin.
6) Scatter the sliced pistachios over the barfi's surface whenever the time is up while still in the microwave and let stay for 10 minutes.
7) Remove the barfi from the microwave after 10 minutes and cut it into 2- inch squares. Cool it down, and then serve it.

⸎ **Indian Rice Pudding**

❖ **Ingredients**

- Half cup of rice
- 3 cups of full-fat milk
- 1 cup of coconut milk
- Half cup of sugar
- Half teaspoon of green cardamom
- One tablespoon oil
- One spoonful of cashews

- One spoonful of pistachios
- One tablespoon of almonds, all nuts should be chopped
- One teaspoon of saffron

❖ **Steps to Follow**

1) Gather all of your ingredients.
2) Soak the rice that you are using it for 30 minutes if you want to reduce the cooking period. Not only does this reduce the boiling period, however, up to half less milk would be used.
3) If you use entire pods of cardamom, smash them coarsely with a pestle and mortar. Add nuts in it and crush it to a fine paste.
4) Add the milk, coconut milk, and the rice into a deep saucepan and carry it to a boil. To steam, reduce the heat and insert the sugar and cardamom. To heat the butter. Stir it continuously.
5) Cook until the rice are smooth, not rubbery, stirring regularly. Based on the rice you have been using, the cooking period would vary around 1 hour. Keep a close eye on the mixture as it heats, and if it is becoming too hot, add some more sugar.
6) Assemble the toppings you want to use and toast the nuts in rice.
7) Let it cool off. And then serve it.

⁜ **Jalebi**

❖ **Ingredients**

- 1 cup of flour
- One tablespoon of chickpea starch

- Powder of ¼ teaspoon cardamom
- ½ teaspoon of baking powder
- ¼ teaspoon of soda
- Five teaspoons of yoghurt
- Food color orange, if you want to
- Water as required
- Fry jalebi with oil or ghee

Syrup for dipping the jalebi

- 1 cup of sugar
- ½ cup of water
- Powder of 1/4 teaspoon cardamom,
- ½ teaspoon of lemon extract

❖ **Steps to Follow**

1) Mix all the ingredients.
2) Focus on a sustainable batter, add food color and water in it.
3) This should not be too dense for the batter. Depending on maida and besan consistency, you can need up to 3/4 of the water.
4) Wrap the batter with foil, and allow the batter to ferment for 10 hours.
5) Whisk a little more of the batter later. If the batter is too thick at this stage, you can need to add a little water.
6) In the meanwhile, add water then add sugar to the mixture to let it all simmer.
7) Let it steam until the syrup is thick and sticky. Basically, put a drop of syrup between your thumb and

forefinger, and it should develop a unified thread as you shift your fingers away from one another.

8) Put the batter in a container.

9) In a pan, heat oil or ghee. Keep the heat down to moderate-low.

10) Squeeze the batter in hot oil, allowing the spiral pass. Note to hold the shape at low heat, or you probably would not be able to form it. If the batter disperses in the oil, it is maybe too thin, and you need to add more flour in it. With the batter, after you have rendered the spiral form, lift the heat to moderate to high.

11) Fry until it becomes crispy. Remove from the oil and dip directly in warm sugar syrup, nice enough for a couple of seconds on either side.

12) Strip the sugar syrup from the jalebis and pass it to the serving tray. Enjoy the homemade jalebi with rabri or milk. You should garnish the top with any almonds.

- **Shakkarpara**
- **Ingredients**

  - Processed flour-2 tassels
  - Ghee -1/4 cup
  - Sugar-1 cup
  - Ghee

- **Steps to Follow**

1) Begin with grinding the processed flour to make the dough for shakarparas.

2) Take processed flour and a quarter cup of melted ghee in a dish. Mix it all together very nicely. Add water in it. You may use warm water during the winters to knead the flour. We used half a cup of water to knead

the same volume of dough. Cover the dough and leave it aside to settle for a half-hour.

3) Then make the dough again after 20 minutes to make it smoother and fluffy. Break the dough into two separate pieces. To avoid drying, take one part and cover the other one. First, form it into a flat dough disc.

4) Take out the sheet being stored. Second, even out the stretched sheet from the corners. Then break it into pieces which are wide. Break the stripes down into long pieces. As required, you may hold the size large or tiny. Now set the shakarparas apart and placed them on a tray. Repeat the process.

5) Heat the oil in a wok enough to fry those. To verify the ghee, drop one piece of shakarpara. We do not need the very hot ghee to fry the shakarparas it ought to be moderately hot. Keep a moderate-low flame. When the ghee is fully hot, drop the rest of the shakarparas into the ghee, too.

6) When the shakarparas rise on the top, flip the sides and begin to fry till they get light golden from all sides. On a pan, strain out the cooked shakarparas. Keep the skillet on the wok's edge, so excess ghee flows back into the wok.

7) Take a container to make a sugar syrup. Add sugar and water in it. Cook until the sugar decomposes. Take some drops in a bowl to sample, then take it in between your thumb and index finger. Check if a long string is shaped when the fingers are spread apart. The syrup is set. Switching the flame off.

8) Over a net stand, position this vessel so that the syrup condenses down a bit. When the syrup becomes small dense in consistency, drop the shakarparas into the sugar syrup and cover them beautifully — taking out the

shakarparas directly from the syrup in a large bowl after combining them in the syrup. In the same container, pour out the excess syrup. You should reheat it a little if the syrup becomes too dense when covering the shakarparas.

9) Stir a spoon of sugar-coated shakarparas to detach them. Otherwise, they would cling to each other.

Chapter 06: Vegetarian Indian Recipes

These days, more people want to eat only vegetarian food rather than Non-veg because most Non-veg dishes raise fat amount in our body and take a long time to get digested because of certain health issues such as obesity, thyroid, weight gain. In this chapter, you will study about some of the vegetarian dishes, which are both nutritious and tasteful.

↓ Vegetable Biryani

Serves to 3 persons

Cooking time: 2 hours

- ❖ **Ingredients**
    - 2 teaspoons of oil
    - One small cauliflower, separated into tiny parts
    - 2 big, peeled and cut into cubes sweet potatoes
    - 1 big onion, chopped
    - One stock of hot veggies
    - One tablespoon of curry paste

- One chili, thinly sliced
- Big pinch of threads of saffron
- One tablespoon of mustard seeds
- 500 g Rice
- 140 g beans
- Two tablespoons of lemon juice
- A couple of leaves of coriander

❖ **Steps to Follow**

1) On moderate flame, heat ghee in a big deep pan. Add the onion, and simmer for around 5 minutes until it softened. Mix the cumin seeds in it; cook it for around 5 minutes, and the cumin seeds start to pop.

2) Add the paste of ginger garlic, onions, and ½ cup sugar in it. Take it to a boil and cook for around 5 minutes until the water is absorbed. Mix the peas, onion, and carrots in it. Also, add all spices in it. Stir carefully, then wrap it with lid and simmer for three minutes.

3) Add 4 cups of water and carry to a cook over medium temperature. Mix rice after boiling, reduce heat to mild, re-heat and cook for 10 minutes. Lower the heat and proceed to cook for another 20 minutes before the rice has softened.

✢ **Indian Sparkling Dhal**

Serves to 4 persons

Cooking time: 1 hour

❖ **Ingredients**

- One tablespoon of oil
- 1 cup sliced onion

- 2 (delicately sliced) garlic cloves
- 1 tablespoon (coarsely diced) ginger
- 4 cups of water
- 1 cup rinsed dried red lentils
- 1 tablespoon cumin
- 1 tablespoon of coriander
- 1 tablespoon of turmeric
- ¼ teaspoon cardamom
- ¼ teaspoon of Cinnamon
- ¼ teaspoon pepper
- Salt as per your liking
- 2 tablespoons of a paste of tomato

❖ **Steps to Follow**

1) Collect all ingredients.
2) Warm the oil over a moderate flame in a medium-sized soup pan. Add the onion, garlic and ginger in it. Cook and keep stirring regularly, for around 6 minutes.
3) Add water, lentils, vegetables and salt. Keep stirring continuously. Carry the soup to a low boil, then switch the heat down to low, cover and cook for around 20 minutes or until the lentils become very soft.
4) Add the tomato paste when well blended. Cook for some more minutes.
5) Serve it and enjoy.

✦ **Koora Cabbage**

Serves to 4 persons

Cooking time: 2 hours

❖ **Ingredients**
- Cooking oil: 3 tablespoons
- 2 chili peppers dried hot, cut into bits
- 1 tablespoon black split skinned lentils
- 1 tablespoon Bengal gram
- 1 teaspoon of mustard seeds
- A few curry leaves
- 1 pinch of powder Asafetida
- 4 peppers of green chili, chopped.
- 1 cabbage head, thinly sliced
- ¼ cup of frozen peas

❖ **Steps to Follow**

1) Heat the oil over moderate-high flame in a broad skillet; cook the red chili peppers, all types of gram mentioned above, and mustard in the hot oil. If the gram starts browning, add the curry leaves and asafetida powder. Stir it well.

2) Add the green chili peppers and proceed to cook for another 3 minutes.

3) Add the cabbage, peas and lentils to the combination; season it with salt; continue cooking until it starts to wilt, but stays a little crunchy for about 10 minutes.

4) Put the coconut into the combination, and simmer for another 2 minutes.

5) Instantaneously serve and enjoy.

✢ **Dhal of Indian with Spinach**

Serves to 4 persons

Cooking time: 2 hours

❖ **Ingredients**

- 2 cups of yellow split peas (approximately 14 ounces)
- 8 cups of water
- Freshly squeezed lemon juice for two teaspoons (from around one medium lemon)
- Kosher salt two teaspoons, plus more as required
- Eight teaspoons butter unsalted (1 stick)
- Two teaspoons of cumin seeds
- 1 ½ teaspoons of turmeric
- 5 big, peeled and finely minced garlic cloves
- ¼ cup of fresh ginger peeled and finely chopped
- 1 medium chili serrano stemmed and thinly chopped
- Spinach, 8 ounces, washed and coarsely chopped

❖ **Steps to Follow**

1) In a fine-mesh strainer, position the split peas and rinse them vigorously under cold water. Switch to a wide saucepan, add the water you have weighed and bring to a boil over high heat.

2) Reduce the heat to medium-low and simmer, occasionally stirring and skimming any scum off the surface with a large spoon until the peas are completely soft and the consistency of split pea soup thickens for about 30 minutes.

3) Set aside, remove from the heat and add the lemon juice and the measured salt in it.

4) Heat the butter over medium heat in a frying pan, until it is foamed. Add the cumin seeds and turmeric in it and simmer until the cumin seeds are toasted and fragrant and the butter is very foamy, stirring periodically, for around 3 minutes.

5) Add the garlic, ginger and serrano; season with salt; and simmer for around 2 to 3 minutes, stirring periodically, until the vegetables have softened. Add the spinach in it and simmer until the spinach is fully wilted, stirring periodically, for around 4 minutes.

6) With the split peas, move the spinach mixture to the reserved saucepan and mix to blend. Serve with steamed rice or naan.

Masoor Daal

Serves to 4 persons

Cooking time: 2 hours

❖ Ingredients

- 2 cups of dry masoor dal, sorted and well rinsed (aka red lentils)
- 8 cups of water
- 1 tablespoon of oil (flavored coconut oil or neutral)
- 1 big, finely diced yellow onion
- 6 cloves of garlic, minced
- 1 tablespoon of minced ginger
- 2 green chilies, minced
- 1 tablespoon of Indian curry powder

- 1 teaspoon of whole seed mustard
- 1 teaspoon of coriander
- ½ teaspoon of cumin
- 1 ½ teaspoon salt or as per your taste
- 1 ½ cups of new chopped tomatoes

❖ **Steps to Follow**

1) In a broad jar, mix the lentils and water. Carry to a boil, then put down the pressure to simmer. Cook it while partly wrapped with lid until the lentils are soft, for about 15-20 minutes normally.

2) Prepare the tadka when the lentils are cooking. Heat a skillet over medium heat and add a pinch of salt, oil and onion, garlic, ginger, chilies. Fry for around 5 minutes until it becomes tender.

3) Add the spices along with the salt, curry powder, mustard, coriander, and cumin. Remove for around 60 seconds to mix and prepare, then add the tomatoes. If frozen, cook the tomatoes for around 7 minutes, or until the tomatoes are soft and saucy.

4) To infuse with spice, add the tadka to the cooked lentils, and simmer over low heat for around 5 minutes.

5) Garnished it with basmati rice and cilantro. And serve.

Conclusion

Indian food can be both thrilling and daunting, with all its exotic products, unfamiliar sauces, and tongue-tingling tastes. It is a complete world of taste. To get a titillating culinary experience, you mix many of the strategies from other cuisines and incorporate mysterious spices. Do not be afraid to start cooking Indian food at home. First, the different dishes and flavors that make up Indian food are important to consider. The food in India is as popular as you can find in Europe. All are entirely new, and the only element that links is a judicious awareness of the usage of spices.

There are 20 to 30 essential spices used in many sauces, such as cumin, coriander, turmeric, and ginger, to name a handful, and there are numerous ways to use them. Spices have cardiovascular advantages, and they also make the meal more tasty and entertaining.

In history, geography and environment, variety can be seen in India's cuisine. Spices are a crucial part of the preparation of food and are used to increase a dish's taste. For the proper preparation of Indian cuisine, accurate usage and combining of the aromatic spices are essential. Also, oil is an essential part of cooking, be it mustard oil in the north or coconut oil in the south. Vegetables differ according to season and area. The vegetables are cooked as a main dish.

Indian Food has an extra advantage for vegetarians. It is one of the most comfortable cuisines around for them. Judicious application of seasoning and sauces bring the taste of potatoes, cauliflower, spinach, and eggplant. Keep things easy at home as you start out.

Made in the USA
Coppell, TX
27 November 2020